SPIDER WOMAN
WALKS THIS LAND

CONTEMPORARY NATIVE AMERICAN COMMUNITIES
Stepping Stones to the Seventh Generation

Despite the strength and vibrancy of Native American people and nations today, the majority of publications on Native peoples still reflect a public perception that these peoples largely disappeared after 1890. This series is meant to correct that misconception and to fill the void that has been created by examining contemporary Native American life from the point of view of Native concerns and values. Books in the series cover topics that are of cultural and political importance to tribal and urban Native peoples and affect their possibilities for survival.

SERIES EDITORS:
Troy Johnson
American Indian Studies
California State University, Long Beach
Long Beach, CA 90840
trj@csulb.edu

Duane Champagne
American Indian Studies Center
3220 Campbell Hall, Box 951548
University of California, Los Angeles
Los Angeles, CA 90095
champagn@ucla.edu

BOOKS IN THE SERIES
1. *Inuit, Whaling, and Sustainability*, Milton M. R. Freeman, Ingmar Egede, Lyudmila Bogoslovskaya, Igor G. Krupnik, Richard A. Caulfield and Marc G. Stevenson (1999)
2. *Contemporary Native American Political Issues*, edited by Troy Johnson (1999)
3. *Contemporary Native American Cultural Issues*, edited by Duane Champagne (1999)
4. *Modern Tribal Development: Paths to Self Sufficiency and Cultural Integrity in Indian Country*, Dean Howard Smith (2000)
5. *American Indians and the Urban Experience*, edited by Susan Lobo and Kurt Peters (2001)
6. *Medicine Ways: Disease, Health, and Survival among Native Americans*, edited by Clifford Trafzer and Diane Weiner (2000)
7. *Native American Studies in Higher Education: Models for Collaboration between Universities and Indigenous Nations*, edited by Duane Champagne and Joseph (Jay) Stauss (2001)
8. *Spider Woman Walks This Land: Traditional Cultural Properties and the Navajo Nation*, Kelli Carmean (2002)

SPIDER WOMAN WALKS THIS LAND

Traditional Cultural Properties and the Navajo Nation

KELLI CARMEAN

ALTAMIRA PRESS
A Division of Rowman & Littlefield Publishers, Inc.
Walnut Creek • Lanham • New York • Oxford

ALTAMIRA PRESS
A Division of Rowman & Littlefield Publishers, Inc.
A Member of the Rowman & Littlefield Publishing Group
1630 North Main Street, #367
Walnut Creek, CA 94596
www.altamirapress.com

Rowman & Littlefield Publishers, Inc.
4720 Boston Way
Lanham, MD 20706

12 Hid's Copse Road
Cumnor Hill, Oxford OX2 9JJ, England

British Library Cataloguing in Publication Information Available

Library of Congress Cataloging-in-Publication Data

Carmean, Kelli, 1960–
  Spider Woman walks this land : traditional cultural properties and the
Navajo Nation / Kelli Carmean.
      p. cm. — (Contemporary Native American communities)
Includes bibliographical references and index.
  ISBN 0-7591-0243-0 (cloth : alk. paper) — ISBN 0-7591-0244-9 (paper :
alk. paper)
  1. Navajo Indians—Social life and customs. 2. Navajo philosophy. 3. Navajo
Indians—Material culture. 4. Cultural property—Protection—Southwest, New.
I. Title. II. Series.
  E99.N3 C344 2002
  305.897'2—dc21
                                          2002001983

Printed in the United States of America

⊗™ The paper used in this publication meets the minimum requirements of American
National Standard for Information Sciences—Permanence of Paper for Printed Library
Materials, ANSI/NISO Z39.48-1992.

CONTENTS

List of Illustrations

Preface

THIS BOOK IS THE RESULT OF my first sabbatical from Eastern Kentucky University. These six months were spent primarily on the Navajo Reservation in northern Arizona. I worked for a month as an official tribal archaeology volunteer out of both the Flagstaff and Window Rock offices of the Navajo Nation Archaeology Department. In this capacity I participated in recording archaeological sites and in conducting traditional cultural property interviews. During the fall semester of 2000, I took courses in Navajo Studies at Diné College in Tsaile, Arizona, including Navajo Tribal Government, Navajo History, Navajo Oral History, Navajo Holistic Healing, and Navajo Rug Weaving. I also began writing this book.

Through seven years of heavy undergraduate anthropology teaching at Eastern Kentucky University, I have become convinced of the need for literature that is specifically oriented to general readers as well as to undergraduates, many of whom may not be anthropology majors. This literature needs to be accessible in the sense that it is relatively easily read by interested, intelligent nonprofessionals. Too often, anthropological case studies contribute to the common problem of not being able to see the forest for the trees. Following good anthropological tradition, great quantities of descriptive detail and copious references are provided without enough emphasis given to central themes. Students, initially excited about learning about a new culture, are often intimidated by the detail and eventually lose interest. Thus, this literature must strike a delicate balance between main theme and detail, where the latter does not overshadow the former, and yet where the issues are not oversimplified. In this book I have attempted to strike such a balance. My main motivation in writing it stems from the belief that if anthropology cannot be made interesting, worthwhile, and at least somewhat conceptually transformative, then something is wrong with our collective anthropological pedagogy.

This literature needs to provide not only sound description of cultural and historical processes, but also needs to serve as an anchor point for understanding important contemporary issues. Students often are more motivated to understand a new culture if there is a specific topical issue woven into the presentation of that culture. Additionally, students need to be provided with a clear point of articulation at which their own culture and the new culture meet. This meeting may be antagonistic or beneficial; the specific nature of the meeting is less important than the fact of the meeting itself. Without a point of articulation, students fumble about in a kind of "cultural vertigo" where they are unable to see the relevance of studying the new culture because it lacks meaning for them. Rather than placing the burden on the student for overcoming his or her own cultural vertigo, it is the responsibility of anthropological pedagogy overall.

Through teaching it has also become clear that students learn best if an entertaining but relevant story is embedded in the lesson. Such stories add a personal dimension to a lecture or a reading that helps paint a visual picture for the learner, thus enabling him or her to relate to the material differently. In an effort to provide this personal dimension here I have included personal journal entries. I did indeed keep a journal during my sabbatical, which included sketches, maps, descriptions of personal experiences, events I attended, factual information, impressions, poems, and emotions. The journal entries included here are in some instances taken almost verbatim from my journal; others are slightly altered and include references, after I made the decision to include such entries in the book. Every entry has substantial basis in my actual experience. The order in which the reader encounters the journal entries is not necessarily the order in which they actually occurred. All of the personal names have been changed.

The journal entries also provide the basis for one of the central themes of the book: continuity and change. Through occasionally fast-forwarding to the present, the reader is able to see how various aspects of Navajo life have remained similar, and how others have changed. The theme of continuity and change is also apparent through the relationship between the prologue and the epilogue—how Spider Woman of the original stories may be understood by Navajo today.

The choice of Spider Woman is deliberate. She is a common and well-known Navajo supernatural entity, with a very prominent home. Anyone who has visited Canyon de Chelly will most likely also have visited her home, Spider Rock, even if they did not realize it. Thus, the choice of Spider Woman and Spider Rock as continuing narrative threads, although perhaps approaching cliché for Navajo scholars, allows the average reader both a geographically and culturally-accessible entry point into both Navajo culture and traditional cultural properties. The chapter heading icons are from spider motif petroglyphs found at Willow Springs, Arizona, and may represent Spider Clan designs (Patterson 1992, 184).

My interest in writing this book centers on two main goals, both directed to undergraduate students as well as to the educated and interested public. The first goal is to introduce the concept of traditional cultural properties. This legal concept centers on the tangible and intangible physical manifestations of our collective experience on this continent. Our collective experience includes Native American creation era events, prehistoric archaeological sites, and the historic period since the European invasion of the continent. I discuss key pieces of legislation to provide the foundation for understanding traditional cultural properties—those locations on the landscape that are important reflections of our collective cultural experience.

The second goal of the book is to serve as a brief but nevertheless stand-alone introductory ethnography of the Navajo. This is a tall order for a short book, particularly given the tomes of written work on the Navajo. Thus, I wish to make it clear that I have made no attempt to create a comprehensive Navajo ethnography. Rather, this work provides an introduction and further reference to other sources that contain further information about Navajo culture as well as other perspectives on Navajo issues.

These two themes meet in this book, and their meeting complements each other. Students can recognize the importance of understanding Navajo culture because it may touch their own activities, through visiting Canyon de Chelly or the Grand Canyon, or skiing at the San Francisco Peaks. Even if students live far from Arizona, they may be able to envision themselves doing such things, or may choose to visit the Bighorn Medicine Wheel or Devils Tower in Wyoming, or even far away Uluru (Ayers Rock) in Australia—all high-profile, traditional cultural properties far from Navajoland. My hope is that the lessons learned from the Navajo context will enable readers to look at their own landscapes differently, and to appreciate the fundamental importance of all such landscapes to different cultures. Thus, this book serves as a springboard toward recognizing the importance of traditional cultural properties, wherever in the world those properties may occur.

In working toward these goals I provide two perspectives concerning traditional cultural properties. One perspective is that of the western, legalistic framework that seeks to manage traditional cultural properties, and the other is the Navajo perspective that creates the traditional cultural property itself. The Navajo perspective appears in the prologue and epilogue, thus bookending the main text firmly in that perspective. I have also sought to keep the reader tied into the Navajo perspective by liberally peppering the main text with reference to the Navajo creation era, even when the text concerns the western, legalistic perspective. My hope is that the reader does not forget the cultural context—whether it be Navajo or other traditional culture—that breathes life into the very same traditional cultural properties that the western, legalistic framework is designed to manage.

I also hope to provide a sense of the difficult-to-escape cultural tension over land management needs that exist among Native Americans, land-based religions, and the federal government, oftentimes concerning identical tracts of land. No easy answers to this cultural tension appear in this book, for there often are none. Although at first this fact may seem disappointing, hopefully readers will come to accept this fact as a reality of the complex world in which we now live.

Chapters 1 and 2 provide a cultural and historical background to the Navajo Indians. Chapter 3 presents Navajo examples of traditional cultural properties. Chapter 4 introduces the concept of traditional cultural properties and the legal background that created the framework to manage such properties. Chapter 5 outlines the current Navajo Nation economy with its focus on natural resource extraction and the substantial royalties that flow into tribal coffers through such extraction. This current economic situation is discussed within the difficult irony that traditional cultural properties—an embodiment of traditional Navajo culture—are often threatened by the very projects that fund both traditional Navajo cultural programs as well as improve the current standard of living for tribal members. Chapter 6 describes how cultural resource management—including traditional cultural property work—is carried out on the reservation. Finally, chapter 7 compares and contrasts traditional cultural properties at various scales, and addresses the difficult issue of material benefit and cultural loss in the Navajo context. This final chapter also broadens the discussion beyond the Navajo context to briefly consider several high profile traditional cultural properties in other North American contexts, as well as in Australia. All Navajo words encountered in this book follow the standard orthography contained in Young and Morgan (1987).

Unfortunately, it is not uncommon for a student in my North American Indians class to ask why Indians need to be treated fairly today, since they were conquered by a technologically superior society. I believe that many, even if voiced by few, share this position. As a teacher, I owe that student a reasonable, well-considered answer, rather than a piercing look of disdain stemming from a sense of political correctness. Indeed, that moment may be my best opportunity of the semester to actually teach that student something truly important.

I suggest several issues for the student to consider. I suggest that the manner in which the dominant society treats its minority members is a reflection of the values of the dominant society. If minorities are treated with injustice, then we are an unjust society. If not all members of our society are allowed to practice their religious beliefs, then we are an intolerant society. Since most of us believe that the United States is founded on justice and tolerance, it is incongruent that the dominant society should treat a minority group—even if they were militarily conquered—with anything other than justice and tolerance. This suggestion encourages students to reconsider their position from a new perspective.

I also speak about the tremendous loss in the number and variety of cultures that exist in the world today. This loss is due to the spread of industrialization into the far corners of the globe, in search of both natural resources and markets for their products. Thus, students are able to understand the unpleasant truth that the loss of world cultures is tightly linked to our own "progress." As traditional cultures—embodied in traditional cultural properties—fall by the wayside and are replaced by the modern, industrially based values of individualism and competition, our world becomes less interesting, more blandly uniform. The loss of world cultures is our communal loss, as cultural diversity enriches the lives of everyone.

By educating students as well as the lay reader about traditional cultural properties as understood from the Navajo perspective, readers are better able to understand the role that tradition plays in the contemporary lives of the Navajo today. A new insight is gained into the tension that exists between economic development, traditional heritage, and cultural resource legislation. This insight, in turn, allows these individuals to recognize and support the need for progressive legislation—and the consistent application of that legislation—that enables our society to be both just and tolerant. This new perspective can only help Navajo people as new policies, procedures, and agendas that are set impact their lives and culture both on and off the reservation.

Royalties from the sale of this book go to the Native American Scholarship Fund, sponsored by the Society for American Archaeology, to support Native Americans and Native Hawaiians in their pursuit of degrees in archaeology.

Acknowledgments

I OWE MANY PEOPLE thanks for the publication of this book. Thanks to Barbara Mills for helping get the whole project going. Thanks to Tony Klesert and Miranda Warburton, both of the Navajo Nation Archaeology Department, who enabled me to spend time in the field. Thanks also to a number of Navajo friends and teachers at Diné College who accepted me so gracefully into their lives. Special thanks to Roger Anyon, who read and commented on an early version of the manuscript and was a terrific sounding board throughout the entire process of research and writing. Thanks also to my father, Willard Carmean, who read the manuscript with a fine-toothed comb. And finally, thanks to Mike Chinquee for his willingness to search for spider icons at the drop of a hat.

Prologue: Spider Woman Walked This Land

FROM THE HEIGHTS of the white-capped Spider Rock, the Spider Woman, *Na'ashjé'ii 'Asdzání*, watched as the two Navajo women approached Canyon de Chelly. Among the Navajo, Spider Woman was known to throw her web to capture and devour disobedient children. Indeed, everyone knew that the white stains on the top of her rock were the sun-bleached bones of her young victims. Yet the two approaching women also knew that Spider Woman often responded with kindness and goodwill to troubled humans. As they approached her home, the women recalled a legend in which Spider Woman had assisted the Twins in their pursuit of the terrible Monsters that had plagued the Navajo people.

It is said that long, long ago, Monsters roamed the Fifth World and fed upon the five-fingered Earth Surface People, today called the Navajo. Each time the people began to settle in an area, building homes and preparing fields for crops, the Monsters attacked and killed many, forcing the defenseless survivors to flee in search of safety. So frequent were the attacks that soon the Navajo were few in number, had taken to hiding, and were desperately frightened.

It was in their time of greatest need that Changing Woman, impregnated by the Sun, gave birth to the Twins. Seeking to help their people by killing the Monsters, the Twins set off on a journey to visit their father and request his aid. Soon they met Spider Woman, a small and often overlooked creature, but one with great power. Spider Woman helped the Twins by teaching them protective prayers and by giving them hoops tied with sacred life-feathers, the power-filled plumes plucked from living eagles. On the trip to their father's home, the Twins entered Peach Canyon, near the southern end of present-day Lake Powell. Peach Canyon was the home of the Crevice Monster who crushes anyone who enters. Only with the use of the prayers and life-feather hoops provided by Spider Woman were the Twins able to escape the crashing walls and continue their journey. After testing

Figure 1.   Original painting by Brandon Milford, *Changing Woman and the Twins.* Courtesy of the Office of Navajo Government Development, *Navajo Nation Government Booklet, Third Edition.*

the Twins to prove their identity as his sons, their father the Sun gave them powerful lightning bolt arrows and other magical weapons to slay the Monsters.

Using the weapons provided by the Sun, the Twins killed *Yé'iitsoh,* the Giant Monster, by inflicting a deep and fatal knife wound. As the blood flowed from the wound it created a huge, craggy expanse of rock near *Tsoodził,* now better known as Mount Taylor in New Mexico. This huge, flowing rock formation fills the entire valley to this very day.

Yet the death of Yé'iitsoh did not end the danger for the Navajo because other Monsters still roamed the land. The older Twin, who came to be known as Monster Slayer, continued the quest to make the Fifth World safe for the Earth Surface People. The younger Twin, who came to be known as Born for Water, stayed with his mother, Changing Woman. Born for Water recorded Monster Slayer's successes through collecting parts of the Monster's dead bodies as trophies.

With the help of Gopher, who dug a tunnel through which Monster Slayer could safely approach *Déélgééd*—the sleeping Horned Monster—the elder Twin killed another fearful beast that had long preyed upon the Navajo. Monster Slayer then began searching for the Bird Monster to destroy it also. As he traveled toward the Monster's rocky cliffs, the Twin heard the flap of wings above him. Three times Monster Slayer successfully dodged the Bird Monster as the feathered beast swooped from the heights, attempting to grab his prey. But the fourth time Bird Monster dove from the sky, the great bird clutched Monster Slayer in his talons and carried him toward the cliff where the young Monster Birds awaited their next meal. It is the fall from far above into the nest of the hungry bird children that had killed the previous victims of Bird Monster, and the Twin seemed doomed to the same fate. Yet, at the last moment, Monster Slayer remembered the sacred life-feather hoops that Spider Woman had given him. It was this precious gift that saved him from death and allowed him to kill the Bird Monster. Monster Slayer continued his quest to rid the Monsters from the land, and finally made the Fifth World safe for the five-fingered Earth Surface People.

Thus, it was the good-hearted Spider Woman who helped the Navajo people by assisting the Twins in ridding the world of the flesh-eating Monsters that once roamed the earth. It was this long-ago benevolence that the two Navajo women now recalled as they walked further into Canyon de Chelly in search of the deity's home.

As Spider Rock loomed large in their path, the women's thoughts concerned the present troubles facing the Navajo. Although the Twins had slain the Monsters long ago, the Navajo still faced difficulties, for winters were harsh in the country in which they had settled and the people suffered from hunger and cold. Desperate to help their people, these women now searched for the same divine being that had assisted the Twins so long ago. The women hoped that Spider Woman would help them once more.

When the two visitors drew near Spider Rock, Spider Woman cast her web and lifted the wary women to the summit of the rock. Here she taught them how to weave. First, Spider Woman built a loom. Then she taught the women to shear the wool from sheep, to clean and card the wool, to spin the wool into yarn, and to dye the wool with colors from the world. Finally, Spider Woman taught them to weave the yarn into a rug while holding beautiful thoughts in their minds and putting their whole souls into their work. Weaving day after day, the women soon became adept at the art, but as they worked they wondered how this new knowledge could possibly help their people. Not understanding Spider Woman's true intent, and feeling disappointed in their efforts to assist their people, the women deliberately created a flaw in the design. They also left an opening in the weaving so that their souls could escape.

Upon discovering the imperfections in the rug, Spider Woman's anger was quickly tempered with compassion as she instructed the women to return to their homes. As they left, they were deeply disappointed and convinced of their failure to help their people with their winter hardships. To ease their discouragement, they taught others the skills they had learned from Spider Woman. Eventually, the people became skillful weavers, providing themselves with beautiful rugs to keep warm in winter and a surplus with which to trade with their neighbors for food and animal skins. Thus, through the efforts of Spider Woman, the Navajo people learned to weave, and as a result, to stay warm during the cold winters and trade for valuable goods. Spider Woman, from her home at Spider Rock in Canyon de Chelly, had once again helped her people.

The Early Navajo   I

HE NAVAJO CREATION STORY describes how the Navajo people emerged from one world to the next (Gill 1983; Newcomb 1990; O'Bryan 1956; Reichard 1934; Zolbrod 1984). The story details how the five-fingered Earth Surface People, the *Nihookáá' dine'é*, or simply, the *Diné* (the People), formed traditional clans and came to inhabit the present Fifth World. It is this world that the Twins cleansed of Monsters by utilizing the life-feathers provided by Spider Woman (Mullett 1979). How does the entry of the Navajo into the Fifth World, as expressed through oral narrative, correspond with their arrival in the Southwest as understood by anthropologists? Through linguistic evidence, it is clear that the Navajo and the Apache, their close linguistic cousins, are relative newcomers to the American Southwest. But just how new are they? What is the evidence—both anthropological and from traditional oral narrative—for the timing of their arrival in the Southwest? Anthropologists believe that when the ancestors of the Navajo first arrived in the Southwest they were primarily hunter-gatherers, but when the Spanish wrote their first observations of the Navajo in 1630, they were described as horticulturists. Archaeologists believe that the ancestors of the modern-day Navajo learned farming, as well as other cultural traditions, largely from the Pueblos. But how, when, and where did this information exchange take place? The answers to these and other questions are still hotly debated.

Based on archaeological and linguistic evidence, several different human migrations are believed to have entered North America across the Bering Strait from Siberia (Downs 1984). The earliest waves of migrants were the Paleo-Indians, entering North America around 15,000 years ago, if not earlier. The modern descendants of Paleo-Indians include the vast majority of Indian people in North, Central, and South America. A second migration stayed far to the north, and the modern descendants of these people include the Aleut and Inuit of the Arctic.

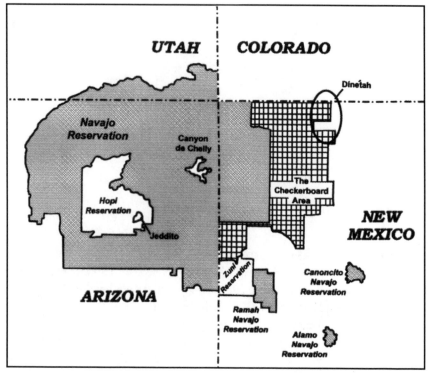

Figure 1.1.   Map of the Four Corners Area of the Southwest.

The Navajo and Apache are members of a larger language group called the Nadene. The Nadene speakers crossed into North America somewhere between 3,000 and 6,000 years ago (Haskell 1987). As such, the Navajo and their linguistic cousins are not only relative newcomers to the Southwest, but to the North American continent as well.

For unknown reasons, once Nadene speakers entered North America, they began separating and moving in various directions (Brugge 1983; Dutton 1976; Haskell 1987; Hoijer 1971). The Navajo are classified as members of the Athapaskan branch of Nadene. Contemporary linguistic relatives of the Navajo are found in the Pacific Northwest—the Eyak, Tlingit, and Haida. Present day Alaska and Canada are home to the Northern Athapaskan language family, and include such subarctic Indian groups as the Beaver, Han, Hare, Ingalik, and Kutchin. As part of these migrations, the ancestors of the Navajo and Apache split off from the northern body of Athapaskans and moved southward. In their southward movement their language diverged from that of their northern brethren, and became known as Southern Athapaskan. As Athapaskan speakers in the Southwest,

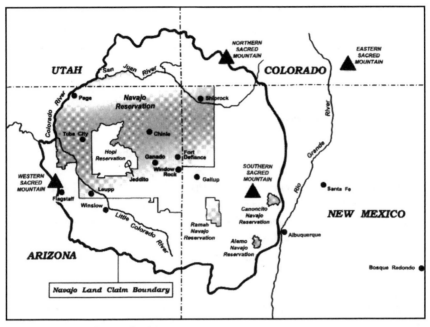

Figure 1.2.   Map of Navajoland.

the Navajo and Apache today are separated from their linguistic kinsmen to the north, and are surrounded by speakers of other tongues.[1]

The timing of the Southern Athapaskan language split is not clear. Using glottochronology,[2] the split occurred around 1,000 years ago (Haskell 1987, 19). Based on linguistic similarities and differences between various Northern and Southern Athapaskan groups, it appears that Southern Athapaskan speakers may have moved off from the north as one large unit, rather than in small groups over a long period of time.

Estimated dates for the arrival of the Southern Athapaskans in the Southwest also vary, as does the route taken—either through the High Plains or the inter-montane areas west of the Rocky Mountains. Based on tree-ring dates from northwestern New Mexico, archaeological evidence places Athapaskan arrival from around 1450 A.D. at the earliest, to the mid-1500s on the late end (Towner 1996). Navajo oral narrative, however, clearly places the Navajo in the Southwest much earlier than does current archaeological evidence. Oral narrative describes the Navajo as occupying the area during the same time that many Anasazi (Ancestral Pueblo)[3] archaeological sites were still inhabited. In some instances Navajo oral narrative even refers to the initial construction of buildings at a specific site, for example Pueblo Bonito in Chaco Canyon, suggesting the Navajo were in the area well *before* the Anasazi left the region by 1300 A.D. (Faris 1990; Kelley and Francis 1998; Warburton and Begay 2000). The Navajo emergence story identified the manner and the location (probably an alpine lake in present-day southwestern Colorado) in which they arrived in the Southwest, but when might this emergence have occurred? Overall, based on oral narrative handed down through the generations in highly conservative ceremonial contexts, the Navajos consider themselves to have been present in the Southwest much earlier than many archaeologists would be willing to accept.

Archaeological evidence suggests that the ancestors of the Navajo were originally hunters and gatherers, but they may have absorbed some knowledge of the buffalo hunting and horticultural practices of the Plains and Intermontane Indians during their southward migration. Perhaps the most significant innovation the migrants brought with them was the sinew-backed bow, a much stronger and more formidable weapon than the simple wooden bow used by the Pueblo cultures already established in the Southwest (Brugge 1983; Kluckhohn, Hill, and Kluckhohn 1971). At some point either on their southward trek or even after their arrival in the Southwest, the Navajo added conical dwellings of wood and earth, later called forked-stick hogans, to their original Athapaskan culture (see Jett and Spencer 1981 for a discussion of hogan architecture with photographs). Remains of forked-stick hogans can be found in Dinétah—the birthplace of the historically recognizable Navajo culture. (See figure 1.3 for a historic hogan, and figure 1.4 for a contemporary hogan.) It is here, in northwestern New Mexico near Farmington, that archaeologists have recognized the earliest, positively dated material remains that can be unambiguously attributed to the Navajo (Towner 1996). Again, however, it is important to note that the archaeological identification and dating of these material remains does not mean that the Navajo had not already arrived in the Southwest at an earlier date.

On a field trip for my Navajo History class, we took a very long day trip to Dinétah, led by my instructor, a Navajo man named Steve. We all piled in a van and headed east over the Chuskas, taking the partially paved road over beautiful Buffalo Pass. Forked-stick hogans are some of the most visible remains of the early Navajo in Dinétah. A casual hiker would very likely pass these by, or worse, collect the remains as firewood. Since we were with Steve, he led us directly to many of these former homes. Once they were pointed out to us, the forked-stick hogans were clearly recognizable as such. Old, sun-bleached cedar branches—the long-since-collapsed hogan walls—lay on the ground like rustic star bursts. The ancient hogans were small in comparison to modern hogans, only measuring around five or six feet across. Oftentimes, they occurred in small groups, perhaps representing the home of an extended family. Broken pottery and the debris from making chipped stone tools was scattered all around. Some faintly burned areas may have been all that now remain of old cooking

Figure 1.3.   Laura Gilpin, *Hogan in Red Rock Cove*, nitrate negative, 1932, © 1979, Amon Carter Museum, Fort Worth, Texas, bequest of the artist.

hearths. We also saw early Navajo pictographs—painted rock art—whose motifs can be linked with modern Navajo ceremonies, suggesting that Navajo religious concepts had come into clear focus at least by Dinétah times, if not earlier. When we visited these pictographs, several people, including Steve, pulled out their small leather pouches and quietly sprinkled cornmeal offerings on the faded red, white, and yellow painted images.

Figure 1.4.   Author's photograph of modern hogan.

We also hiked to the top of Gobernador Knob, the birthplace of Changing Woman. Steve put us all to shame, nearly running to the top of the Knob while the rest of us panted away, wondering when we would finally get there. Scattered around the base of the Knob were frequent and quite obvious concentrations of broken plain-ware pottery, presumably early Navajo. Our instructor told us these were offerings to the supernatural beings that inhabited the Knob, both then and now. At the top of the Knob we could see for miles in all directions. Neither Gobernador Knob nor the areas around it are on the Navajo Reservation. Rather, the land is publicly owned, administered through the Bureau of Land Management, which leases large tracts to natural gas companies. From our vantage point we could both see and hear the gas being sucked out of the ground all around the area below the Knob.

Pottery offerings were scattered over the top of the Knob as well. Steve told us that Navajo medicine men were supposed to make regular visits to these sacred places, and make offerings to them, but that such visits were rarely made anymore. He said that Pueblo medicine men still came to the Knob to make offerings, and that he has seen their prayer sticks—carved wood and feathers wrapped in cloth—nestled under boulder overhangs. His opinion was one I had heard many times before: traditional Pueblo culture has been more resilient in the face of culture change than has the Navajo. After appreciating the view and observing other important landmarks, Steve announced he was going to make an offering, and if anyone wished to join him, they could. Four of us—about half our group—chose to participate. He lined us up facing east, said a brief, quiet prayer in Navajo, and sprinkled cornmeal toward the east.

Once the Athapaskans arrived in the Southwest, they came into contact with the various Pueblo Indian groups who farmed and lived in permanent, sedentary villages. It was at this time that the Apache and Navajo, both Southern Athapaskan speakers, began to split from one another. The Apache maintained a more mobile, hunting and gathering lifestyle, while the Navajo began to incorporate many of the subsistence and cultural features of their new Pueblo neighbors.

Raiding and violence appear to have been endemic in much if not all of pre-contact North America, and the Southwest was no exception. The appearance of the horse, brought to the Southwest by the Spanish in the mid-1500s, increased the effectiveness of raiding. Raids might be conducted in retaliation for the death or capture of a loved one. Raids were also conducted to gain or retrieve material goods, food, livestock, and human captives. Captives obtained in raids were adopted, used in a mild form of domestic slavery, or sold to the Spanish, and later Mexicans, as slaves. Over time, slave raiding increased as the value for slaves rose higher and higher. The Navajo were as likely to be victims of these raids as they were to be the perpetrators.

Although they continued to hunt, the Navajo also cultivated crops, including corn, squash, and beans. As farming gradually became more important the Navajo moved from the nomadic lifestyle adaptive to hunting and gathering to a more sedentary existence. Through trade, intermarriage, and conflict, the Navajo adapted other traits from the Pueblo (Brugge 1983; Dutton 1976; Hester 1962, 1971; Waters 1950). Examples of these traits include the development of clans, matrilineal descent, and matrilocal residence. In fact, oral clan histories, many of which were recorded in the late 1880s, indicate that fully 15 percent of contemporary Navajo clans have Anasazi and/or Puebloan origins, suggesting that contemporary Navajo are a highly genetically and culturally mixed group (Warburton and Begay 2000).

Today, Americans determine descent using both the father's and mother's relatives, a system anthropologists call bilateral descent. However, there are two other major means of defining membership in a kin group. One is through the father's line (patrilineal descent) and the other is through the mother's line (matrilineal descent). We know that at European contact, Northern Athapaskan kinship was bilateral—thus suggesting the Navajo underwent rapid cultural change upon their arrival in the Southwest, since the Navajo were matrilineal at European contact, and remain so today.

Postmarital residence patterns describe where the newly married couple will reside. In Anglo-American society today, neolocal residence is the norm, where the couple establishes a new home apart from both sets of parents. Patrilocal residence is where the new couple resides with the groom's family. Matrilocal residence is where the new couple resides with the bride's family. From an anthropological perspective it is important to understand that both descent and postmarital residence patterns are not at all static. These highly flexible kinship patterns reflect how a culture adapts to its environment, its dominant subsistence system, and with surrounding cultures. At European contact, newly married Navajo couples lived with the bride's family—matrilocal residence—and the groom paid a brideprice to the woman's family, similar to kinship and residence patterns of many Puebloan groups.

My first day of classes at Diné College, not too surprisingly, involved introductions. What was surprising, however, was that those introductions also involved a person's clans. The order of clan introductions is very specific. First, students identified their mother's clan and since the Navajo are matrilineal they were thus identifying their own clan. Then, they identified their father's clan, which by definition is different from their own since Navajos must always marry outside their clan, and preferably outside their father's clan, or even outside a group of closely related clans. Each student also identified their mother's father's clan, and their father's father's clan. Each student's four clans are then known to everyone present, so that their relationship to everyone else can be determined. Karen, a woman who would become my good friend, introduced herself in this way: "I am 'Áshįįhí (Salt Clan) born for Tó Dích'íí' (Bitter Water). My maternal grandfather's clan is Tábąąhí (Edge Water) and my paternal grandfather's clan is Tł'ízíłání (Many Goats)." She mentioned later that clan-wise, she and our instructor were brother and sister to each other. At least in theory, this kind of relationship defined their behavior toward one another.

When it came time for me to introduce myself—the only Anglo in class—I felt like a complete orphan, since I have no clans. The contrast was stark: Anglo society does not place as much importance on kinship—a group identity that stretches back into the mists of time—but rather on one's individual identity, often expressed as personal educational accomplishments or career attainments. Feeling utterly silly but nevertheless wanting to express some kind of family connectedness, I muttered something about my mother's side originating in England and my father's side originating in France, fully realizing that in mainstream Anglo society one would never introduce oneself in such a manner. My classmates did not seem to think this was silly, however, and no one ever batted an eye when I did it on many other occasions. Since that time I observed several clan introductions by mixed blood Navajo. In such instances, a part Navajo and part Anglo individual, for example, would insert Bilagáana (White person)[4] at the appropriate places in the recitation, without any hint of embarrassment, for there was none; this was information exchange that served to place an individual in a broader group context.

The clan introductions I heard were almost always in Navajo, even when the rest of the introduction, such as where a person was from, was in English. Only once did I hear a clan introduction in English, and that was when the person stumbled around for awhile in Navajo, and then gave up and said her clans in English; most Navajo who speak only English can usually still manage to pull off the rote recitation of their clans, memorized specifically for such formal occasions. Even though I don't speak Navajo I learned to recognize several of the more common clan names to the point that I could tell when clan introductions were being made. I observed that such introductions occurred frequently, especially among adults, and were made very quickly upon meeting a stranger.

Navajo clans are said to have originated in the creation era. After the Twins had slain the Monsters, their mother—Changing Woman—left to live on an island in the sea to the west. After a while she became lonely and decided to return. On her way back from the west she decided to create people to keep her company. She created people by rubbing the outer layer of skin from various areas of her body and thus begetting a variety of clans. These people eventually multiplied and went in different directions, themselves splintering off to form different clans. The clans were named through events they experienced, or distinguishing character-

istics of the original clan founders. For example, the Salt Clan, of which my friend Karen is a member, was so named when—long, long ago—the Navajo raided a nearby pueblo close to a salt lake and captured two girls, bringing them back as slaves. Eventually, the many descendants of these two girls became known as members of the Salt Clan. Since members of the Honeycombed Rock Clan captured the girls, these two clans are closely related, and their members cannot marry one another (Zolbrod 1984:337). At least sixty clans exist today, some with few members and others with many (Witherspoon 1983).

Older Navajo complain that the younger generation is losing its clan focus. Indeed, some traditional people complain that some younger Navajo have even married within their own clan, which is incestuous. However, high school yearbooks on the reservation today sometimes list the maternal clan following an individual's name, and graduations often call out the clan names of the graduates. Obituaries in the newspaper always identify clan affiliation. The clans of individuals running for political office will be specified in the introductory paragraphs of newspaper articles. Thus, despite some recent changes, it is clear that the principle of matrilineal kinship remains strong among the Navajo.

Other cultural traits incorporated from the Anasazi and/or Pueblo include certain religious beliefs and ceremonial paraphernalia, including the use of cornmeal and corn pollen in ceremonies, the use of gourd rattles, fox skins as tails, woven cotton kilts, and masks in some dances. Navajo and Pueblo religion is clearly distinct in many ways, however. Navajo religion, for example, has its emphasis in the restoration of health to the individual, whereas the emphasis of Pueblo religion is on the common good (Haskell 1987:96). Thus, although the Navajo adopted many aspects of Pueblo culture, as well as vice versa, it is important to recognize that the Navajo clearly did not simply import these traits without change. Rather, a new, hybrid culture emerged, a creative blending of Pueblo and Athapaskan traditions adapted to the Southwestern environment, spawning a unique culture all of its own.

The Spanish Period

In 1540, Francisco de Coronado's expedition arrived in the Southwest (Acrey 2000; Forbes 1960). The expedition was composed of 225 cavalrymen, 60 footmen, 5 Franciscan friars, and nearly 1000 African slaves and Mexican Indian servants. The party brought with them approximately 1500 head of livestock including horses, mules, cattle, sheep, and swine. They came with hopes of finding vast amounts of gold and silver, as earlier Conquistadors had done in Mexico and Peru. As Coronado entered the Southwest, the ancestors of the present-day Navajo were still mostly in northern New Mexico—Dinétah—in the formative stages of the evolving Navajo culture (Keur 1944; Towner 1996). Although the Navajo probably had no direct encounter with Coronado, it is not difficult to believe that they heard both of his arrival as well as the expedition's violent encounters in many Pueblo villages.

Finding no silver or gold, Coronado did not stay long. After two disappointing years he withdrew to Mexico with heavy losses. The failed expedition, however, left important vestiges of its passing. For the Navajo, the early adoption of sheep would cause major economic and cultural changes, such that when the Spanish later returned, the Navajo had very successfully added sheep herding to their already mixed subsistence system of horticulture, hunting, and gathering. Once again, through the rapid adoption of pastoralism, the Navajo had adapted their culture and lifestyle to new opportunities, thus demonstrating that the ability to be flexible in and of itself was advantageous. With Coronado's departure, crown-sanctioned Spanish expeditions to the Southwest ceased for some fifty years. During this time, however, numerous unofficial Spanish slave raids into the Southwest occurred, setting in motion a vicious cycle of slave raiding and counter-raiding that would continue for some three hundred years.

Disease was another important vestige of Spanish entry into the Southwest (Dobyns 1991; Reff 1991). Since crossing into North America over the Bering Strait, New World Indian populations had no contact with their long-ago Asian ancestors. During this lengthy separation, new and deadly infectious diseases had developed in Old World towns. Even though new strains would periodically emerge as epidemics and result in much agony and death, Old World peoples, having lived with these endemic diseases in their populations for thousands of years, had slowly developed a partial natural immunity to these diseases. The genetically isolated peoples of the New World, however, had no natural immunity to these diseases. Smallpox, measles, tuberculosis, and influenza were the major European-introduced diseases that devastated Native American populations across the entire hemisphere. These diseases appeared as epidemics, killing untold thousands of people over the course of several centuries. In some areas, as much as 90 percent of the population may have died during these epidemics. At times whole Indian ethnic groups ceased to exist, while the tattered remnants of other groups merged with neighbors to form new, coalescent tribes.

In the American Southwest—then referred to as northern New Spain— Spanish documentation of aboriginal population is not nearly as extensive as it is for other areas such as Central Mexico and Peru. Puebloan population estimates suggest these sedentary peoples may have numbered over 100,000 in 1598, when the first colony was founded (Reff 1991, 22–30). By 1638, only around 40,000 Puebloans appear to have been alive; by 1660, the population had been reduced to around 24,000, and only twenty years later to only 17,000. Overall, these figures represent an 80 percent decline from the early 1600s to 1680. No clear population figures exist for the Navajo and Apache, who would have been particularly difficult to count given their dispersed, more nomadic lifestyle. Thus, it is difficult to assess European disease impact on these Athapaskan groups, although it undoubtedly severely impacted these cultures as well.

In 1598, the Spanish Crown sent a colonizing expedition to the Southwest with the aim of establishing a permanent presence in the area. Juan de Oñate's colonizing party ousted Puebloan peoples from their villages to provide the new colonists with dwellings. He set up a system of Indian taxation based on tribute, both in the form of goods and labor, for the construction of new Spanish communities such as Santa Fe, Oñate's capitol. Oñate also began the systematic conversion to Christianity of the Puebloan peoples through harsh tactics such as destroying kivas—their underground ceremonial rooms—and physical punishments for Puebloan religious leaders. Because of such tactics, many of these religious leaders took refuge with the Navajo during this period of persecution, thus accelerating the exchange of cultural and religious traditions between the Navajo and Pueblo (Brugge 1983).

After tolerating over eighty years of harsh Spanish rule, the Pueblos, in an uncharacteristically unified move, rebelled against their overlords. The 1680 Pueblo Revolt killed around 400 Spaniards. Around 2000 escaped to Mexico, where the colonists waited until they were able to exact revenge on the Pueblos. The wait would be brief. Only twelve years later, the Spanish reconquered the entire Rio Grande valley. Numerous Puebloan people again left their villages and sought refuge among the Navajo, again accelerating the interchange of traditions (Kelley and Whiteley 1989; see Keur 1944, and Powers and Johnson 1987 for archaeological documentation of Navajos and Pueblos living side by side). Even today there remains a large amount of intermarriage between Navajo and various Pueblo groups.

When the Spanish first arrived they only made very simple distinctions among the wide varieties of Indian groups they encountered. Coronado only distinguished the sedentary Pueblos from the more nomadic *Querechos* that populated much of the eastern Southwest and the western Plains. Later Spaniards began to recognize differences among these groups and adopted the word *Apachu* (enemy) from the Zuni for the more nomadic Indians closer to the Rio Grande pueblos. To the Spanish, these people were simply bothersome raiders that existed on the periphery of the sedentary Pueblo world. The year 1626 saw the first written documentation of the realization that the Apache and the Navajo were different (Dutton 1976). A Franciscan friar, Zárate Salmerón, wrote that some Apaches were actually farmers, and called them *Apaches de Návaju*. The word "Navajo" is derived from a Tewa Pueblo word for "great cultivated fields," reflecting the Tewa's understanding of the distinctions between these two groups. Thus, at least by 1626, if not earlier, the Navajo had become a clearly recognizable culture by both the local Indians as well as by the Spanish.

It is also clear that the Spanish concentrated their attention on the Pueblos, rather than on the Navajo or other more nomadic groups (Acrey 2000; Terrell 1970). Numerous reasons exist for this "preferential" treatment. First, since the Pueblos were sedentary, they were much easier to find and control than the highly mobile Navajo. The Pueblos lived in densely populated, permanent villages, whereas the Navajo maintained a dispersed, mobile settlement pattern necessary for grazing sheep. This scattered settlement pattern meant that huge areas of land would have to be covered to round up only a small handful of Indians. In many ways the Pueblos were sitting ducks waiting for the Spanish to pluck. Second, Pueblo population was much greater than that of the Navajo, thus providing a larger labor force for Spanish needs. Additionally, since the Pueblos were primarily farmers rather than practicing the mixed subsistence strategy of the Navajo, they were able to produce more food for the Spanish, particularly in those Rio Grande pueblos where irrigation was practiced. The Navajo also fought the Spanish very differently than did the Pueblos. Since the Navajo were already highly mobile, when Spanish military expeditions came to seek revenge for Navajo raids, the Navajo simply retreated, melting into the landscape. Indeed, the Navajo would successfully use this very effective fighting strategy for over 200 years. Puebloan warriors, while putting up valiant resistance to Spanish military campaigns, ultimately had few retreat options other than nearby Pueblo villages. Finally, environmental factors played a role in the Spaniard's essential avoidance of the Navajo. Much of Navajo territory was quite rocky, which meant that Spanish horses quickly lost their shoes and became lame. Since horseshoes were expensive and hard to come by in the young colony, expeditions against difficult enemies had to be carefully considered. Overall, the Spanish viewed fighting the Navajos to be a lot of trouble for not very much gain, and thus a losing proposition.

As a result, the Navajo were largely disregarded by the Spanish. Even though the first Catholic mission for the Navajo was built in 1629, it was very small and quickly failed. The next mission was not built until 1749 and was abandoned one year later. Not until 1898, thirty years after the Navajo returned from their confinement at the military encampment at Bosque Redondo, was the first successful mission built. This mission, St. Michael's near Window Rock, Arizona, is still in operation. In contrast, many of the Pueblos, particularly those along the Rio Grande River, have had continuously functioning churches in their communities since the Spanish Reconquest, and Catholicism and Pueblo culture have blended together in now inextricable ways (Kessell 1989).

Even though the Spanish largely ignored the Navajo, it does not mean the Navajo were spared from conflict. Throughout this time the Navajo were victims of slave raids from Utes, Comanches, Kiowas, and Spaniards acting outside of official Spanish law. Although Spain had forbidden the enslavement of Indians, Spanish colonists felt free to ignore a mandate handed down from far across the Atlantic. Political leaders in the colonies supported the slave trade and the majority even actively participated. Sometimes the leaders kept the Indian captives in their own households, other times they gave the slaves away to gain political favors or to strengthen friendships. Although slave raiding was endemic to much of pre-contact Indian society, it increased greatly with the arrival of the Spanish, as they were ever-willing buyers and required vast numbers of slaves to work the silver mines of Mexico (McNitt 1972). To complicate the picture even more, periods of friendly trade relations beneficial to all existed as intervals of peace alternated with raiding. Thus, life in the Southwest was hardly peaceful or predictable from anyone's perspective.

Prior to and following Spanish arrival, the Navajo political system was characterized by numerous, localized headmen, *Naat'áanii*, who led based on their personal abilities (Downs 1984; Kelley and Whiteley 1989; Wilkins 1999; Witherspoon 1983). Often these individuals accumulated great wealth according to Navajo standards, and may have had a number of wives. These headmen had no coercive authority, but rather relied on persuasion to influence the behavior of others. While these individuals were certainly respected by their followers, the followers themselves were under no obligation to obey their headman's wishes. In anthropological terms, this kind of political organization is termed *egalitarian* and is based on the "achieved" status of the headmen, stemming from their own personal talents and abilities.

Before European contact and indeed well into the 1800s, there was no political entity that could be described as the Navajo "tribe." The highest degree of political unity that occurred was a periodic, regional assembly of local headmen, called the *Naachid* (Wilkins 1999). This gathering was a combination of ceremony—dancing and prayers for good crops—and political discussions, attesting to the interwoven nature of religion and politics. Women could speak freely at these gatherings and Naachid decisions were not binding on anyone present. The last Naachid was reportedly held in the 1850s or 1860s, before Navajo removal to Bosque Redondo. The overall lack of political unity can best be seen in raiding patterns: Navajo were just as likely to raid other Navajos as they were to raid Pueblos or other Indians (who were equally likely to raid the Navajo). Although all Navajo people shared a common language and culture, they were not politically unified and thus did not act as one group until the reservation era.

Coming from a stratified society where leadership was based either on hered-ity or formal appointment, the Spanish, Mexicans, and later the Americans were unwilling to accept the uncertainties of the egalitarian Navajo political system. The colonists wanted Indian leaders who could speak for the entire tribe, make treaties, enforce decisions, and punish those individuals who did not abide by the treaties. In an optimistic but futile effort to change the Navajo political system, first the Spanish and later the Americans simply appointed political leaders for the Navajo. Not surprisingly, the colonists appointed those individual Navajo head-men who were amenable to Spanish demands.

In 1786, the Spanish appointed Don Carlos, the first in a long line of ap-pointed Navajo "chiefs" (Acrey 2000). Don Carlos was a headman from the Ce-bolleta area of New Mexico—which was much closer to the major Spanish set-tlements of Albuquerque and Santa Fe than were the majority of Navajo—who had by this time moved west into northeastern Arizona, in part to escape repeated slave raids. Due to the proximity of the Cebolleta band to the Spanish settlements, Don Carlos, as well as subsequently appointed "chiefs," firmly believed that the Spanish were too strong a force to fight and that the only hope the Navajo had for survival was to forge a peace with them. Living closer to the Spaniards, it is likely that this group bore the brunt of Spanish retaliatory raids. Not surprisingly, the appointment of Don Carlos as "chief" was not recognized by the main body of Navajo.

By 1818, while the Mexicans struggled to gain their independence from Spain, the Navajo's internal schism was solidified when Joaquin, also of the Cebolleta band, was appointed "chief." From this point on, Joaquin separated his band from the rest of the Navajo in order to independently negotiate a peace. His band even fought alongside the Spanish, and later the Mexicans, against other Navajos. Bit-ter over this betrayal, the Navajo gave Joaquin and his band the name Diné 'Ana'í (Enemy Navajo). The motives of the Diné 'Ana'í are often debated (McNitt 1972; Trafzer 1982). Some scholars argue that the Enemy Navajo sued for peace because they considered fighting the Spanish fruitless; others contend that Joaquin and his followers aligned themselves with the Spanish for self-gain, profiting from the in-creased access to livestock and slaves. Under several different leaders, the Diné 'Ana'í served as scouts and soldiers for the Spanish, and after 1821, for the Mex-icans. They would also fight with the next group to seek control of the Southwest, the Americans, thus contributing to the final military defeat of the Navajo.

After an eleven-year struggle, Mexico gained its independence from Spain in 1821, yet that seemingly momentous event held little significance for the Navajo. Many Spaniards—now Mexicans—who had previously participated in the slave trade remained in power and continued their involvement in the illegal but lucra-tive trade. Meanwhile, important new arrivals had appeared in the Southwest. In a very brief period of time these individuals were to change Navajo life more profoundly than the Spanish had done in almost two hundred years.

The American Period

As landless immigrants from Europe flooded the eastern seaboard of the newly independent United States, the concept of Manifest Destiny became firmly established in their ethos: the ownership of the entire North American continent was seen as their God-given right. Spurred on by land developers, these immigrants bought newly divided land and took up homestead leases, encroaching further and further west. By the early 1800s, westward European migration had arrived in the Southwest.

As victors in the Mexican-American War and with the signing of the Treaty of Guadalupe Hidalgo in 1848, the United States gained control of 55 percent of Mexico's territory. These lands included all of present-day New Mexico, Arizona, California, and Texas, and parts of Nevada, Colorado, and Utah. Initially, many Navajo assumed that because the Americans had been enemies of the Mexicans they would be allies of the Navajo. As the Anglo-American and Navajo cultures clashed, however, it was clear this alliance would not occur any time soon. In particular, the Americans were enraged by continued raiding, which had long since become an established way of life for all Indians of the Southwest. The Americans promised the Hispanic residents that they would put a stop to Navajo raids, which were taking a heavy toll on nonnative settlements in the area. Initially, punitive expeditions by American forces were no more successful than had been the previous Spanish and Mexican maneuvers (Downs 1984; Trafzer 1982; Underhill 1956), but this was soon to change.

Placed in charge of the military operations in New Mexico in 1851, Colonel Edwin Sumner led his force deep into Navajoland, and built a fort they intentionally named Fort Defiance. A later fort, Fort Sumner, would be named after this man. The Navajo, recognizing the futility of attacking the large and well-built Fort Defiance, remained peacefully and quietly in their small, dispersed settlements, herding their sheep. While a frustrated Sumner and his troops marched through the heartland of Navajo territory, Navajo living near the edges raided New Mexican settlements in his absence. The civil authorities demanded that Sumner strengthen his force with New Mexican volunteers, but, to his credit, Sumner refused. The experienced military leader recognized that the use of these volunteers, deeply involved in the ongoing slave raids, would only serve to intensify hostilities. Rather, Sumner insisted on placing responsibility for the continued conflict on both sides. As a result of Sumner's policy, a brief peace existed during the winter of 1851–52, but by the spring of 1852, hostilities once again broke out (Trafzer 1982).

The situation again briefly quieted when the governor of New Mexico appointed Henry Lafayette Dodge as Indian agent to the Navajo. Dodge traveled throughout Navajo territory without military escort, encouraging an end to the hostilities. He was genuinely concerned for the welfare of the Navajo, and unlike the agents before him, he lived and worked among the Navajo, thus earning their respect. Between 1853 and 1856, Dodge worked to maintain peace and to contest the encroachment of New Mexican stockmen and raiders into Navajoland. Unfortunately, the much-admired agent was killed by Apaches while hunting in 1857, and the largely peaceful conditions in New Mexico ended that same year (McNitt 1972; Trafzer 1982; Underhill 1956).

During the American Civil War, Union military strategists sent additional troops and volunteers to the American Southwest to counter Confederate forces there. With the rapid departure of Confederate forces from the region, General James Henry Carleton, military commander of the New Mexico Territory, devised a plan to utilize both the now-idle regulars and the New Mexican volunteers in a military campaign against the Apache and Navajo. Carleton considered it his duty to civilize and Christianize the Indians, and his plan was to subdue and capture members of these tribes and imprison them at Bosque Redondo, a location in eastern New Mexico expressly chosen for this purpose.

Kit Carson's Scorched Earth Campaign

One of Carleton's first moves after his appointment as military commander was to choose Lieutenant Colonel Kit Carson, former mountain man and previous Indian Agent in New Mexico, to conduct a military campaign against the Apache and Navajo. Carson secured members of the Ute tribe—bitter enemies of the Navajo—as scouts. New Mexican volunteers, anxious for the opportunity to attack the Navajo and perhaps steal away some slaves in the process, hurried to enlist. Thus, leading a combined force of Indians, volunteers, and regulars into Navajoland, Carson initiated a campaign that permanently altered the lives of all Navajo. This scorched earth campaign directly led to the forced removal of perhaps half of the Navajo people from the land the Twins had made safe, and where Spider Woman lived (McNitt 1972; Trafzer 1982; Underhill 1956).

The Mescalero Apache were the first target of the campaign, and many Apaches fled to Mexico rather than subjugate themselves to the attacking American force. Fairly rapidly, Carson and his soldiers rounded up the approximately 400 Mescaleros remaining and herded them toward Bosque Redondo. With this accomplished, the campaign then focused on the Navajo in the fall of 1863.

In the early stages of the campaign in Navajoland, the troops captured or killed only a few Navajo, as most simply "melted" into the landscape in their well-honed and practical tactic that had proved successful for hundreds of years. Although Carson had gained a reputation as a skilled scout and Indian fighter, he repeatedly failed to locate the Navajo. The Navajo, on the other hand, would suddenly emerge from their hiding places and attack groups of soldiers and supply trains and frequently succeeded in scattering or capturing the army livestock herds. Nevertheless, these small successes failed to alter the overall course of the war, as the new American military strategy employed against the Navajo was particularly effective.

The American "scorched earth campaign"—crafted by Carleton and implemented by Carson—was not dependent upon killing or capturing the Navajo. Rather, almost exclusively the New Mexican volunteers and regulars relentlessly burned crops and destroyed livestock, intentionally creating a situation to induce Navajo starvation in the upcoming winter. Carson's command also burned hogans and the belongings inside including clothing, blankets, stored food, and other possessions. The military's goal was to keep the Navajo moving, give them no time to plant crops or build homes, and leave them nothing to return to. Indeed, the mass destruction of Carson's military campaign has been compared to Sherman's march to the sea in the American Civil War. As desired, the Navajo—men and women, children and the aged—felt the pains of hunger as they faced the harsh winter of 1864.

In spite of the arduous conditions they were forced to endure, some Navajo refused to surrender. Many, including Barboncito, an important leader, sought refuge inside Canyon de Chelly, where they hoped to survive undetected. The hopes of this group were in vain, however, for an American force reached the canyon in August 1864 and burned homes, corn crops, and more than 3,000 mature peach trees.

It seems that whenever Navajo talk today of Kit Carson's scorched earth campaign, the thing they mention the most is Canyon de Chelly and the burned peach trees. When I visited Canyon de Chelly, there are few reminders of the many tragedies that occurred there. Indeed, peach trees, some said to be descendants of the original trees, still grow in many places in the canyon. Navajo hogans still dot the landscape, as do cornfields and the moving masses of small sheep herds. Although some Navajo still live in the canyon, they only do so in the summer. During the cold winters they return to their more modern homes on the canyon rim or in the nearby town of Chinle. Tourists are asked not to photograph the private Navajo homes on the canyon bottom. Meanwhile, Spider Rock, the home of Spider Woman, one of the most photographed rock formations anywhere in the country, is almost exclusively seen and photographed from the canyon rim.

Dirt roads crisscross the canyon floor, bringing in both Navajo and flocks of Anglo tourists on jeep tours, affectionately known as the "shake and bake" tours. In addition to farming and sheep herding in the canyon bottom, many Navajos also come down and set up makeshift tables to sell their goods. One can purchase many wonderful items directly from their Navajo makers: silver and turquoise jewelry, dried cedar berry necklaces strung with glass beads, and small sandstone slabs recently hand painted with images of Kokopelli— called Water Sprinkler by the Navajo—the most recognizable and commonly reproduced rock art motif in the entire Southwest.

Today, the Navajo's beloved canyon is owned by the Navajo Nation but is administered by the National Park Service. In 1931, Canyon de Chelly National Monument was created to manage the crowds and to tell the canyon's sad story. A small visitor center has displays and a reconstructed Navajo hogan for tourists to enter. Perhaps because of its astounding natural beauty—transposed against the backdrop of astounding human tragedy—Canyon de Chelly and her peach trees have evolved into a vital symbol of both Navajo suffering and endurance, and Anglo-American injustice.

The military campaign against the Navajo began in 1863, and there is considerable debate concerning how long the policy continued (Jett 1974). Certainly, the effects of the campaign were felt long after it had actually ceased. Gradually, in small, ragtag groups, the Navajo began to surrender. U.S. policy had achieved its aim—the forced removal of the Navajo from their land. In large part this removal was meant to end the continuous cycles of slave raids and counterraids that were causing continued violence and chaos in the Southwest. Unfortunately for the Navajo, the Americans did not uniformly curtail such raiding in all quarters, particularly among the New Mexicans, and the raiding against the Navajo continued. It was clear to the U.S. government, however, that it would be much cheaper to support the Indians on reservations than to fight them. Confining the Indians to reservations would also clear the way for a boom in nonnative settlement of the entire Southwest. Fueled on by land speculators and the continued flood of European immigrants, Indian reservations seemed to make both economic and political sense.

The Long Walk and Bosque Redondo

For one and a half years following the scorched earth campaign, small groups of Navajo would surrender themselves to forts or even to cavalrymen in the field (Acrey 1998; Bailey 1964, 1970; McNitt 1972; Trafzer 1982). Although the period immediately after the military campaign is referred to as the Long Walk, more correctly there were actually a series of long walks, taking different routes, led by different military men, and composed of differing numbers of Navajo. In all, there may have been around twenty long walks, with anywhere from 30 to 2,500 Navajo in each. The walks averaged about 12 or 13 miles a day, making the nearly 500-mile march last just over a month. Conditions varied greatly on the walks, with some military men being exceptionally cruel, shooting anyone who could not keep up. Some were intent on making the Navajo suffer miserably, making them march many miles out of their way to humiliatingly parade them through the streets of Santa Fe. Others tried to make the trek as tolerable as possible for the Navajo given the reality of few rations, few wagons, and few blankets.

Stories of the Long Walk are kept alive through oral tradition (U.S. Department of Education 1990). Many Navajo people have grandparents or other relatives that went on the Long Walk. Throughout these stories runs a common thread—the mistreatment of any Navajo incapable of keeping the dictated pace of the walk. The following story, one of many, provides an example.

> On the journey the Navajos went through all kinds of hardships, like tiredness and having injuries. And, when those things happened, the people would hear gunshots in the rear. But they couldn't do anything about it. They just felt sorry for the ones being shot. Sometimes they would plead with the soldiers to let them go back and do something, but they refused. This is how the story was told by my ancestors. It was said that those ancestors were on the Long Walk with their daughter, who was pregnant and about to give birth. Somewhere . . . south of Albuquerque, the daughter got tired and weak and couldn't keep up with the others because of her condition. So my ancestors asked the Army to hold up for a while and to let the woman give birth. But the soldiers wouldn't do it. They forced my people to move on . . . "Go ahead," the daughter said to her parents, "things might come out all right with me." But the poor thing was mistaken, my grandparents used to say. Not long after they moved on, [the girl's relatives] heard a gunshot from where they had been a short time ago . . . a soldier came riding up from the direction of the sound. He must have shot her to death. That's the way the story goes. (Howard W. Gorman, from Johnson 1973, 30–31).

The place to which the Navajo were walking was Bosque Redondo—*Hwééldi* (the Place of Despair). Bosque Redondo was a vaguely defined area officially one mile in all directions from the central flagpole of Fort Sumner on the Pecos River in eastern New Mexico. Unofficially, the Bosque spread out over a twenty-five mile area and was inhabited by the largest group of Indians ever concentrated together in the history of the Southwest (Acrey 1998). There was no need for a fence, since the isolation, harsh environment, and nearby marauding Indians ensured that the Navajo, for the most part, stayed at Bosque Redondo. The Bosque was an experiment designed by General Carleton, whose goal was to stop the endemic raiding in order to open land up for white settlement, with minimal cost to the government. Overall, some 3,000 Navajos died either during the Long Walk, or at Bosque Redondo during the four years of incarceration.

Between 1864 and 1868, just over 8,000 Navajos were taken to Bosque Redondo. This number was much greater than the military had expected; their resources were overwhelmed and their facilities incapable of dealing with so many people, especially a people already worn down both physically and psychologically from Kit Carson's campaigns and the Long Walk. Although Carleton's plan was to have the Navajo build irrigation canals and grow their own food, this plan was never successful and the crop failed each year. Completely dependent on the government for food, Navajo rations were tight. Local Anglo merchants, knowing they had a monopoly for government supplies in isolated eastern New Mexico, price-gouged the Army, providing a minimum quantity of food for maximum prices. Navajo oral histories tell of eating flour crawling with bugs and boiling shoe leather for meat because they had no choice.

> Another thing, at ration times they would be given one slice of bread. At times, they would kill a rabbit or a rat. If a rat was killed, the meat, with the bones and intestines, would be chopped into pieces, and twelve persons would share the meat, bones and intestines of one rat.[5]

As can be imagined, many problems existed at Bosque Redondo. The Navajo joined an estimated four hundred Mescalero Apaches, traditional enemies of the Navajo, also confined to the reservation. The Diné 'Ana'í were also there; indeed, since they put up no resistance, they were the first to go to the Bosque. Thus, it was difficult to sort out who were the worst enemies—likewise incarcerated Indians or the U.S. Army. Slave raiding against the Navajo continued and any Navajo that wandered just a little too far in search of firewood was picked up by Kiowas and Comanches lying in wait. The Navajo, of course, were weaponless. The Navajo built makeshift hogans from whatever local materials they could gather; cutting wood was not allowed. A lack of proper housing and firewood made the cold winters unbearable. Since rations were so low, starvation was a constant threat. Malnutrition led to illness, which led to widespread death. Infant mortality was high. The sources of disease included a contaminated water supply, which induced malaria, typhoid fever, severe and often fatal cases of diarrhea, and the spread of contagious diseases such as the mumps epidemic of 1864–65.

The large number of deaths was difficult psychologically for many reasons. First, the Navajo were forced to remain near the places where people had died, and thus where ghosts remained. In their sparsely populated homeland, where hogans were easy to construct and mobility was not restricted, ghosts had been easily avoided. Added to this was the tumult of emotional confusion as Carleton at-

tacked Navajo culture in his attempt to permanently force them into a western European mold. Their emotions must have ranged from fear to anger to hopelessness
as they turned to their time-honored methods of handling problems only to find
the traditional ways forbidden, often with the use of violence. The Navajo were
faced with a battle for cultural survival—a struggle they continue to this day.

*I visited Fort Sumner National Monument one July morning, before it got too hot. Paul, the
ranger at the visitor center, at first thought I might be in the wrong place, that I was really
trying to find Billy the Kid's grave site, nearby, down the other dirt road. After spending several hours talking with Paul and visiting the site, he told me that upon realizing they are in
the wrong place, most visitors, if polite, will hurriedly look around Fort Sumner's small exhibits, and then make a beeline for Billy's grave. This made him sad, because Fort Sumner
represents an incredibly important period in our nation's history, one that affected huge numbers of people and changed the lives of their descendants forever. Although Billy the Kid may
be interesting, his life was nowhere near as significant as what occurred at Fort Sumner and
Bosque Redondo.*

*Today, there is little that remains of Fort Sumner, and even less of Bosque Redondo. A
number of the Fort's walls have been partially reconstructed, and a new flag post has been
built in the Fort's small central square. A trail to the river brought me to the quietly flowing, very shallow Pecos River, nestled in a sandy riverbed. Tall cottonwood trees grew from
both banks, and a hawk sailed overhead. It looked like a great place to live, for a small hunting and gathering band, at least. It was clear that 8,000 people trying to live at a place like
this would overrun the local resources in a matter of days.*

*Fort Sumner National Monument was created by executive order in 1968, the 100th
anniversary of the signing of the Treaty at Fort Sumner. In 1971, the Monument was
opened to the public with a dedication by Navajo medicine men. As part of the dedication,
the medicine men created a rock pile travel shrine with rocks from Navajoland. The shrine
has been added to over the years with rocks, twigs, flowers, and other offerings placed there
by Navajo people. A Blessingway ceremony accompanied the dedication, conducted with the
goal of cleansing the area of the 3,000 souls of the Navajo who died there, thus making it
safe to visit. Despite this ceremony, Paul told me that only sixty of the eighty-eight fifth
graders from Newcombe Elementary School on the reservation were allowed to come on a
field trip to Fort Sumner. The parents of those children allowed to attend the field trip demanded that a Blessingway ceremony be conducted by the school prior to the trip. Clearly,
the extreme tragedy of Hwéeldi is still strong in Navajo collective memory.*

It is also important to recognize that not all Navajo left the homeland of Spider Woman, Changing Woman, and the Twins. Several thousand Navajo may have

Figure 1.5.   Author's photograph of Navajo rock shrine at Bosque Redondo, Fort Sumner, New Mexico.

remained in hiding, spreading further west and north to Navajo Mountain, the Grand Canyon, and Utah (Acrey 1998). In hiding, these Navajo adapted to their new conditions by again becoming more mobile hunter-gatherers, building less permanent homes, and planting fewer cornfields. Some of the groups eventually surrendered, while others never did, and were still in their homeland carrying on the old ceremonies when their kin returned from Bosque Redondo many years later.

The Treaty of 1868

The Bosque Redondo experiment was not without its non-Indian critics. Many felt that Carleton's solution to "the Indian problem" was not only too harsh, but also too expensive, particularly given that the Navajo did not appear ready to become self-sufficient any time soon. Beginning in 1867, Congress initiated several investigations into life at Bosque Redondo. The eventual results of these investigations included Carleton's removal as the military commander of New Mexico Territory and the transfer of Indian reservations from the War Department to the Department of the Interior (Kappler 1972).

The Navajo were initially presented with the plan to move to a reservation in Oklahoma, joining numerous other tribes who had been removed there. The Navajo refused this option, successfully holding out for a reservation in their own homeland. Finally, on June 1, 1868, the final Treaty was signed.[6] Although the federal government and the Navajo had made other treaties in the past, either they were never ratified by Congress or the treaties were broken before the ink could dry on the paper. The Treaty of 1868 was the last and final treaty between the Navajo and the United States government. Signing for the Navajo were Barboncito (head signer), Armijo, Delgado, Manuelito, Largo, Herrero, Chiqueto, Muerto de Hombre, Hombro, Narbono, Narbono Segundo, and Ganado Mucho, all making their X mark. Signing for the United States government— *Wááshindoon*—were William Tecumseh Sherman and S. F. Tappan, both Indian Peace Commissioners.

With the signing of the Treaty of 1868, a legal document then and now, the Navajo returned to their beloved homeland, but with numerous restrictions. The first and foremost restriction, contained in Article I, was that the Navajo remain peaceful and cease a raiding way of life. Article II defined the land reserved for the Navajo. This initial reservation land straddled what would later become the New Mexico/Arizona state line, and encompassed about a quarter of their original territory.

Although the land reserved for the Navajo was clearly defined in the treaty, no fence was ever built to define it on the land. In fact, the Navajo never adhered to their original reservation. Instead, due to a livestock herding lifestyle characterized by a high degree of mobility, the Navajo immediately began spreading out to occupy much of their former homeland. Given the vacant nature of the land, the lack of boundary enforcement did not at the time appear overly important, although the long-term results were to have significant impact on the Navajo. Initially Presidential executive orders and later Congressional acts would add more land to the reservation over subsequent years, making legal what was already fact. Beginning with the first land addition in 1878—a mere ten years after the treaty was signed—eight major land additions were made. Rapid population growth—from less than 15,000 when the treaty was signed to well over 200,000 today—was the stimulus behind these land additions. Including the checkerboard,[7] the Navajo Reservation today encompasses some 16,000,000 acres, making it the largest Indian reservation in the United States (Linford 2000). In receiving a large reservation in their own homeland, the Navajo have been relatively fortunate in their dealings with the United States government in comparison with other Indian tribes.

In their expansion, however, the Navajo also began occupying land closer and closer to the Hopi villages. In 1882, an executive order defined a block of land to be set aside for the Hopi "and such Indians as the Secretary of the Interior should indicate" (Acrey 1998, 96; see also Brugge 1994). Prior to 1882 there was no actual reservation defined for the Hopi, who had never moved from their mesa-top villages and thus had never entered into a treaty with the government. The language of the 1882 executive order was to be the basis for a vast array of lawsuits, many brought by the Hopi, which form the basis of what has come to be known as the Navajo–Hopi Land Dispute. From the Navajo perspective, the other "such Indians" were clearly the Navajo, and as such they were entitled to live in the 1882 block of land. From the Hopi perspective, they wanted clear boundaries defining their land, and the right to control who lived on their land. Stock reduction beginning in 1934 brought the simmering land dispute to a head. The dispute was further fueled by Peabody Coal's successful exploration and strip mining of coal on Black Mesa, in the disputed 1882 block, which brought the possibility of new wealth to both tribes.

Amidst numerous lawsuits and court decisions concerning the Navajo–Hopi Land Dispute, three stand out. In 1974, the Navajo–Hopi Land Settlement Act (Public Law 93-531) was passed. This law divided the 1882 block into two geographically equal portions creating the current, serpentine-like Hopi Reservation borders with Jeddito Chapter, a Navajo enclave, in its eastern section. Peabody's permit areas were also equally divided among the Navajo and Hopi tribes. All Navajo living on Hopi land were to be relocated to Navajo land, and all Hopi living on Navajo land were to be relocated to Hopi land. The problem was that there were by far many more Navajo living on Hopi land than vice versa, and that the Navajo Reservation was already quite full and could not accommodate more livestock grazing on their already overgrazed land. Also, the Navajo to be relocated had lived on what was now defined as Hopi land for many generations, and had developed spiritual connections to the land and considered it rightfully theirs. Relocation, often to Anglo border towns, has meant considerable heartache (see Joe 1998 for an account of Hardrock Chapter's relocation experience). Although through the years thousands of Navajo have been relocated, a number of Navajo families have refused to move, and continue to fight relocation.

The second piece of legislation that stands out is the 1980 law authorizing Congress to pay for the costs of relocation (Public Law 96-308). In 1985, another law authorized the Bureau of Indian Affairs to purchase new reservation lands for relocated Navajos near Chambers, Arizona (Public Law 99-190). Nahatá'Dziil (New Lands) was officially added to the reservation in 1991 (Navajo Nation Government, Office of Navajo Government Development).

One weekend I went to my friend Karen's home for a visit. Karen is a nontraditional student at Diné College, returning as an adult to get a college education. Her goal is to get elected as a local chapter official and make some much-needed changes in her community. She has made many sacrifices to return to school, selling her livestock, for example, to get enough money to pay for tuition. She lives in two dorm rooms with her two daughters, ages seven and thirteen, eating in the college's cafeteria.

Karen's home is Red Lake/Tonalea, right at the northwest tip of the recently defined Hopi Reservation. In fact, I could have thrown a stone from her front door to the new barbed-wire fence demarcating Hopi land. By sheer luck, Karen was on the Navajo side of the new border. The land specified in her grazing permit, however, was halved. Federal relocation funds compensate people who had to move, but no compensation was provided for people like Karen, who were certainly impacted by the establishment of new reservation borders, but were not actually relocated. She took her battle to the Navajo–Hopi Indian Commission on Relocation (later renamed the Office of Navajo and Hopi Relocation), and after many, many years of legal battles, was awarded relocation money to build a home. Today, Karen and her girls live in a nice, 1200 square-foot home. They painted it blue.

Nevertheless, politically, Karen lives at the end of a dead end street. Although the dirt road accessing her home continues on into Hopi land, Karen will likely never receive services. There is no water line to Karen's home and she told me there probably never would be. Over the weekend we took the old farm truck to her mother's hogan, where the water line stops. Here we filled up the big plastic tank in the bed of the pickup, and hauled it back to fill the cistern at her house. No electric line goes to her home, and probably never will. Solar panels, bought with relocation money, provide electricity. The entire weekend, no one took a shower, and lights were always turned off when not in use—we watched a video in complete darkness.

Although the Navajo and Hopi tribal government representatives have been at each other's throats for several decades, the people themselves have mostly continued to live peacefully side by side. Indeed, if I hadn't known about the land dispute beforehand, and known to ask questions about the issue, it would have been easy to miss. In places where Navajo and Hopi communities are in close proximity to one another, Navajo and Hopi children attend school together, and intermarriages are still common. I attended a Home Dance in the village of Hotevilla on Hopi's Third Mesa. A Home Dance is where the kachinas *(Hopi supernaturals) that have been living in the village throughout the winter return to their home in the San Francisco Peaks. Throughout the day, brightly costumed and masked kachinas dance periodically in the village's main plaza. A quietly festive atmosphere permeated the village. Snow cone and dill pickle vendors were scattered along the main routes. The onlookers sat on assorted plastic chairs and benches around the plaza edges and on all the roofs of the surrounding homes. Despite the hot August sun, I sat on a roof to get a good view, and over the course of the day struck up casual conversations with onlookers near me. To my surprise, many of the people I talked with were Navajo who either had relatives in town, or had also come simply to observe the dancing.*

The Treaty of 1868 also made clear the political relationship between the Navajo tribe and the federal government. By officially recognizing the Navajo with

a formal treaty ratified by Congress, a direct government to government relationship between two sovereign nations was established. Indeed, through the act of
writing treaties or making executive orders that created reservations, all federally
recognized tribes have a similar government to government relationship. State governments do not have legislative authority over tribal lands. For this reason, tribal
members do not pay state income or property taxes, and tribes are able to build
casinos on tribal lands.

In addition to confirming tribal sovereignty, however, the treaty also reduced
it. Although reservation land was set aside for Navajo use, the Navajo do not actually own title to the land. Rather, the land is held in trust by the federal government for the Navajo. However minor this distinction may at first sound, it is
actually of critical importance and will be addressed again later. As a sovereign nation the Navajo also retain control of most internal affairs, with notable exceptions. The Major Crimes Act of 1885, for example, defined those crimes that
would fall under federal jurisdiction even if committed on tribal land. These
crimes include murder, manslaughter, rape, assault with intent to kill, arson, lar-
ceny, incest, robbery, child abuse, and misuse of tribal funds. The Federal Bureau
of Investigations has jurisdiction over these crimes, while the tribal government
has jurisdiction over all misdemeanors. Limited sovereignty—nation within a nation status, but as defined in the Treaty and subsequent laws—while good in theory is problematic in actuality. Limited sovereignty has created a continual jock-
eying for power between the tribe and the federal government, making for
perpetually tense relations.

Certain promises and requirements were also made in the Treaty of 1868. The
Treaty provided livestock, corn seed, and farming tools. It made western education mandatory for children between the ages of six and sixteen (Prucha 1979).
It promised the construction of schools, a carpenter shop, a blacksmith shop, and
churches. Hunting rights were protected, and welfare and other social services were
guaranteed for poor Navajo. The Treaty also authorized Indian Agents to live on
the reservation to oversee treaty implementation and compliance. Thus, in exchange for peace and ceded land, the federal government entered into a legal and
permanent relationship with the Navajo people.

Notes

1. Non-Athapaskan languages in the American Southwest include Uto-Aztecan,
Kiowa-Tanoan, Yuman, Keresan, Zuni, and Seri (Hale and Harris 1979).

2. Glottochronology studies the rate of language change. Under conditions of minimal interference, language change occurs at a relatively predictable and known rate of
around 20 percent for every 1,000 years. Knowing this rate allows linguists to estimate
when languages split from one another. Since Navajo and Apache are linguistically very

similar, these two groups split very recently (Hoijer 1971). Indeed, Navajo can understand much of the Apache language and vice versa. However, not all anthropologists and linguists trust the reliability of glottochronology.

3. The Anasazi is an archaeologically recognized culture of the Four Corners area of the American Southwest. The Basketmaker Anasazi have been identified as far back as 1000 B.C., and may have evolved out of local Archaic roots. Puebloan Anasazi occupied this area beginning around 750 A.D. and are the architects of such well known sites as the Mesa Verde cliff dwellings and Chaco Canyon. Around 1300 A.D. the Anasazi left the Four Corners region and moved further south, coalescing into the historically known Pueblos of the Rio Grande and Western Pueblo areas. The archaeological term "Anasazi" is derived from the Navajo word 'Anaasází, which is variously translated as "enemy ancestors" or "ancestors of the aliens."

4. Originally, Bilagáana meant something like "man with long white hands and arms," referring to the long white gloves that covered the forearms of the U.S. cavalrymen. Today, the word is generally understood to mean "white people."

5. Mose Denejolie, from Johnson 1973, 243.

6. The Treaty can be read at Harrison Lapanie Jr., "U.S. Treaty with the Navajos," <www.lapahie.com/Dine_Treaty.html> (accessed February 24, 2002).

7. The checkerboard represents a very unusual situation characterized by very complex landholding patterns. In the late 1800s, various railroad companies owned land near their track lines. Navajo soon came to occupy these lands as well, which were slowly given to the Navajo Reservation by executive orders. In an attempt to remedy the situation, the federal government exchanged public land near the reservation for the land given over to the Navajo by executive order. The railroad companies were given the odd sections, while the even sections were opened to settlement by private white ranchers through the Homestead Act, or were given in allotments to Navajo. This odd- and even-section land ownership pattern created a checkerboard appearance on maps. Thus, the checkerboard area is a complex mixture—reservation land, land allotted to private Navajos, private Anglo land, land owned by various railroad companies, federal Bureau of Land Management land, and state land.

Return to Navajoland 2

FTER THE JUNE 1 SIGNING OF THE TREATY OF 1868, the Navajo prepared to return to their homeland. They returned to Navajoland just as they had departed—walking. On June 18, the first and largest return group moved slowly out of Fort Sumner, a column stretching ten miles long.

As the column neared Fort Wingate, near present-day Gallup, New Mexico, three small but important groups split off from the main return party. Two of these groups were composed of the Diné 'Ana'í. Even during the four-year stay at Fort Sumner, these internal divisions did not heal, and these Navajo split off from the main body and went to live on their own, eventually becoming known as the Cañoncito Band. Another group of Diné 'Ana'í split off and headed south, eventually becoming known as the Alamo Band. The Ramah Band also emerged at this time, as other returning Navajo went to join relatives who had escaped from Bosque Redondo some time earlier. Today, the Navajo Reservation still includes these three Navajo enclaves removed from the main reservation. Although the Treaty of 1868 did not allow for such splintering and occupation of nonreservation lands, nothing was done to stop it. It was not until the 1940s and early 1950s that the land occupied by these three geographically isolated groups was converted into reservation land.

The main body of Navajo returned to the homeland, and after receiving the promised seed, livestock, and tools, began spreading out over the landscape. Some returned to their old home places while others joined kin in new areas, building new hogans and returning to a traditional life.

I've seen all kinds of hogans here—very old hogans and brand new ones. I've seen men up on top of hogans currently under construction, nailing together the converging rafters with great care. Some hogans are the traditional anthill-shaped hogans, with the entire outside covered with dirt; others are made out of logs, cut in sections and stacked horizontally, with dirt roofs. Some hogan walls are made out of the local sandstone, with dirt roofs. Newer hogans are often made out of plywood—conveniently sized and shaped for the hogan's six-sided walls—with tarpaper roofs. I've only seen a few of the older style, forked-stick "male" hogans that were not made for tourism purposes. I've seen two-story hogans, hogans with a "Hogan Sweet Hogan" sign hanging on the front door, hogans painted to color-coordinate with the home, and hogans with satellite dishes, skylights, and solar panels. I've seen cinder block hogans built into the rectangular architecture of schools, chapter houses, and senior citizen centers.

All hogans, whether old or new, face east, even if that means an orientation away from the other buildings. Many people still live in hogans, especially older people, with the one interior room crammed full with a wood stove, kitchen table, small cooking area, lots of cupboards, and miscellaneous couches and beds. Formal army photographs and children's school pictures hang on any available wall space. Bathing usually occurs out back, in a metal washtub. I've seen hogans used for overflow sleeping space, for storage, as a silver workshop, and a weaving room. A particularly common use for hogans today, however, is ceremonial, as most ceremonies require a hogan, and for the time span of the ceremony, the hogan becomes the focal point for ritual. One thing is certain: hogan architecture is alive and well on the Navajo Reservation.

Some of the Bosque Redondo returnees stayed close to Fort Defiance, forming a group of Navajo that acculturated rather quickly into Anglo life. Indeed, the immediate post–Fort Sumner period saw the beginning of an important social, political, and economic division of the tribe that continues to this day. The "traditional" Navajo were the ones who filtered back into the landscape, returning to their former way of life. These people learned very little English and were uninterested in Bilagáana ways. The Navajo who stayed close to the Fort formed what today would be recognized as a "nontraditional" division. These people often became employed by the Fort, and to do their jobs effectively, they needed to learn English. Thus, they willingly sent their children to the government schools. Christian missionaries converted these Navajo very early and they quickly gave up traditional clothing. These individuals learned not only to abide by, but also to benefit from government regulations.

For the majority of Navajo who returned from Bosque Redondo, changes came more slowly. Probably the most significant change in those early years was the coming of the trading posts (Aberle 1983b; MacPherson 1992b; Reinhart 1999). The trading posts were so quickly accepted that in a very brief period of time they became a basic institution of Navajo life. The posts brought in cloth, iron pots and pans, flour, coffee, sugar, canned goods, saddles, guns and ammu-

nition, and wagon parts. Around 1900, colorful velveteen blouses liberally stud-
ded with silver coins and buttons became the fashion rage for Navajo women.
Traders were always Anglos, but they usually remained on the reservation for
many years, often becoming trusted as friends fluent in the Navajo language. Post
ownership frequently passed down through the generations, with the traders and

Figure 2.1.   Laura Gilpin, *Navaho Woman, Child, and Lambs,* platinum print, 1932, © 1979,
Amon Carter Museum, Fort Worth, Texas, gift of the artist.

their families becoming long-term fixtures in the small Navajo communities that slowly grew up around them.

The trading post was a social institution as well as an economic one. The trading posts served as the focal point for the dispersed Navajo homes, and Navajo people would gather there to hear the news of the day or to gossip. In addition to providing goods, the traders helped their patrons in many other ways. Mail could be sent and received from the post, and the trader offered friendly help with translations and filling out government forms. Since Navajos had little interest in handling or burying corpses, the trader often performed mortuary services and was

Figure 2.2.   Laura Gilpin, *Trader Troy Kennedy Examining Wool at the Red Rock Trading Post,* gelatin silver print, Jul. 2, 1951, © 1979, Amon Carter Museum, Forth Worth, Texas, bequest of the artist.

much valued for this assistance. Relations between Navajos and traders were not uniformly amiable, however, as the traders controlled much of the reservation economy in a colonial and paternalistic manner.

Trade was always based on credit. Throughout the year, surrounding Navajo families would come to the post and acquire the goods they needed. No money changed hands. Instead, Navajo families sold many lambs to the post in the fall, and their accumulated debt from the summer would be erased. The lambs were then transported away from the reservation for sale as meat. In the spring the sheep were sheared, and Navajo families would bring raw wool to the post, and the accumulated debt from the winter would be erased. The trader would then

Figure 2.3.   Laura Gilpin, *Weaver at Long Salt Hogan,* gelatin silver print, 1953, © 1979, Amon Carter Museum, Forth Worth, Texas, bequest of the artist.

pack the wool into wagons and send it off to the border towns where it would be repacked and transported by rail to various eastern cities for processing. There, the raw wool was industrially cleaned, carded, spun, and woven into fabric for local use as well as further shipment to Europe. Thus, via the wool industry in particular, the Navajo entered the market economy of a much larger world.

In addition to raw wool and lambs, finished wool products were also brought to the trading post. Navajo women would weave the wool into blankets that were then traded, used for warmth during the winter, or utilized as saddle blankets. Initially, the colors and designs were quite simple. The traders, in an effort both to gain more wealth for themselves and to provide the Navajo with a higher income, radically changed the goals and practice of weaving. The traders brought in artificial dyes to create more uniform and vivid colors. The transition was also made away from the more utilitarian blanket to the more decorative rug, both for the floor and, increasingly, to be hung on the wall. The traders also designed new, much more intricate patterns that would be more marketable in Anglo cities. Since the traders were spread out all over the reservation, dozens of different regional styles developed (Kahlenberg, Hunt, and Berlant 1972; see Rodee 1977). Ganado rugs were designed with a bright red background while the Two Gray Hills style features earth tones.[1] In 1890, the cash value of Navajo weaving was estimated to be $30,000; in 1931 the value was $1 million (Roessel 1983). Weaving quality increased dramatically, since well-made rugs brought a much higher price from the trader. Some of the better weavers began focusing almost entirely on weaving, as much of a family's income could now be gained

Figure 2.4.   Detail of the Hubbell Trading Post in Ganado, Arizona, cir 1890s. Lorenzo Hubbell is seated, examining a late-style chief's blanket. Photo by Ben Wittick, Courtesy Museum of New Mexico, Neg. No. 16480.

from the steady and constant production of rugs. Navajo women were no longer weaving for themselves and their families, but for a much larger market; the commercialization of crafts had begun, facilitated by the trading posts.

One Saturday morning I visited Hubbell Trading Post, in Ganado, Arizona. Hubbell Trading Post has been operating continuously since 1876, making it the oldest continually operating post on the reservation. The post is now administered by the National Park Services as Hubbell Trading Post National Historic site and operated primarily by the Southwest Parks and Monuments Association.

The night before, Karen and I had attended an all night Yei-bi-chei, a traditional Navajo healing ceremony, getting stuck in the amazingly muddy road three times. Our shoes were barely visible through the dried mud. The park ranger made us slip plastic bags over our shoes and pants legs before he would let us tour the Hubbell home. Once inside the home, I understood why: huge and beautiful Navajo rugs overlapped each other on the floor of the simple wood and adobe home. These were the largest rugs I had ever seen. John Lorenzo Hubbell himself had created their characteristic pattern, Ganado, named after the nearby town; the town itself was named after an important Navajo headman. Handmade Navajo baskets were nailed, sardine-like, to the ceiling beams. Hundreds of paintings, mostly local landscapes or Indian portraits, hung on the walls.

The most impressive thing about the Hubbell home, though, was the dining room set made out of bird's eye maple. There was a table with at least eight chairs, a buffet, and a sideboard. Hubbell commissioned a Cincinnati furniture maker to build the set in 1895, which cost about $10,000. The ranger directed our attention to the corners of the furniture and the hand rests for the chairs: sheep heads, with intricately carved horns encircling their furry faces. Hubbell wanted the source of his great wealth to be clearly visible to all.

The Park now has a newly built visitor center. The center hires two Navajo weavers as live displays, sitting cross-legged in front of their large, upright looms, right in the middle of the shelves full of merchandise. These two women were probably in their seventies or maybe even their eighties, and could speak no English. Luckily, Karen was more than willing to translate, giving me the opportunity to speak directly with one of the old-time weavers. While she continued her weaving, we spoke quietly for about an hour. She told us that she was seven years old when she sold her first weaving, for fifty cents, at a local trading post. Since she was an only child her parents needed her at home to help with the sheep and other chores, and she regretted never having gone to school. She said she was determined that her children receive an education, and she was pleased that they had succeeded in school. Now, she told us, her son and daughter were both professional people in Gallup, and her grandchildren do not speak Navajo, which made her very sad. None of her grandchildren show any interest in weaving. I told her that I was taking a weaving class at Diné College. She was curious that

*I would be doing such a thing, and she asked me many questions about my little rug—its
size, colors, pattern, where I had obtained the wool, and what kind of weft I was using. I
was never so proud of my little rug as in that moment. I still wish I had stopped by to show
it to her after I finished it.*

*On our way back to Diné College, Karen and I listened to a "Navajo Place Names" cas-
sette (Wilson and Dennison 1995). The cassette presented the English, followed by the Navajo
name, for various important landmarks. To our great amusement, even a well-known liquor
store in Gallup was included. Hubbell's Trading Post was also included, and Karen burst into
laughter when she heard the Navajo translation: "Deaf Man's Trading Post." Apparently, one
didn't have to hear well to still make a fortune in the trading business.*

Silver and turquoise jewelry also became a highly sought after trade item (Bedinger 1973; Roessel 1983). Before European contact, Southwestern Indians valued
turquoise highly. Usually, small pieces of the blue-green stone were ground on the
edges, a small hole was drilled, and the resulting bead was strung with stones and
shells for necklaces and earrings. Turquoise was not combined with silverwork until
the craft became commercialized and produced for Anglo tastes. Navajos had
learned silverworking while at Bosque Redondo, if not before. Not surprisingly,
when jewelry production became commercialized, its production changed greatly.
The traders bought and traded the silver—usually in the form of Mexican pesos,
which had higher silver contents than American coins. As with the other traditional
crafts, the traders encouraged jewelry production with the Anglo consumer in mind.

The rise in ownership of personal automobiles in the late 1920s spurred an increase in road construction, including the famous Route 66 from Chicago to Los
Angeles. Both new roads and new cars brought more tourists to the Southwest, in
large part to visit the Grand Canyon. In turn, tourism gave birth to the concept of
souvenirs. The traders assisted the Navajo economy—and their own—by bringing
Navajo crafts to the consumers. Navajo crafts were bought wholesale on the reservation, transported to urban centers, and sold at a high profit for the trader. In addition to weaving and silver and turquoise jewelry production, other crafts that became commercialized included basketry, wrap-around leather moccasins, and
pottery. The commercialization of crafts has also meant the continuation and/or
revival of craft production that may well have died out if the traders had not ener-
gized it through the forces of market capitalism. For example, many Navajos today
are full-time artists and silversmiths who can earn a good living in these endeavors.

The impacts of the Navajo's entry into the market economy would be felt
first and forcefully during the Great Depression, when the value of most goods
plunged dramatically. The spring wool sale, the fall lamb sale, and the sale of
finished wool rugs and jewelry in the between seasons had largely sustained the

Navajo economy since their return from Bosque Redondo. The Great Depression of the early 1930s began irreversible changes in the Navajo's trading post-oriented economy. Anglos, anxious about their declining wealth, were no longer in the mood to purchase rugs or jewelry. By this time, barter had slowly given way to a monetary system, first introduced to the Navajo with cheap metal tokens bearing the stamp of a particular trading post. As these tokens and coins, along with Navajo livestock and crafts, continued to lose their value, the Navajo were no longer able to maintain an acceptable standard of living. Although Navajo wealth was hardly great prior to the Depression, in many ways Navajo culture had flourished and large wealth distinctions had become evident throughout the reservation.

Huge sheep and goatherds, sometimes numbering in the thousands, were a clear measure of that wealth. Raw wool, lamb sales, and commercial-scale rug weaving operations fueled this increase in sheep, leading to dangerous levels of overgrazing (Aberle 1983b; Kelley and Whiteley 1989). By the 1930s and 1940s the rangeland was no longer able to sustain such overgrazing, and erosion from the reservation added to siltation problems for the recently constructed dams that brought hydroelectricity to the newly booming Anglo cities. These problems prompted the federal government to initiate the highly controversial and much-hated stock reduction programs. Government range specialists determined the number of livestock that could be supported on the reservation: 500,000 head of sheep or their equivalent.[2] However, the Navajo were estimated to have around 1,500,000 head of livestock. Clearly, the number needed to be reduced, and drastically. The Navajo were directed to sell requisite numbers of their livestock, and many did. Those that did not eventually had their livestock shot by government agents, causing much emotional and economic trauma. Prior to stock reduction the Navajo lived a fairly mobile life, moving with the sheep herds in search of pasture. After stock reduction the Navajo ceased to be as mobile, for the sheep herds were now so small they could graze within the local area.

Where are all the sheep? When I first arrived on the reservation I was surprised to not see many sheep, but yesterday I learned an important lesson. I was driving back to Diné College at about five o'clock in the afternoon, shortly before sunset. I now try to avoid driving at this hour since late afternoon is the time sheep get brought back to the corral for the night. I had to stop three times in a single hour to let sheep—accompanied by their unhurried shepherd—cross the road. I've certainly seen some sheep during the day, off grazing on the sparse grass and sage, although they're easy to miss if you're not looking out the window that exact moment. The sheep close to the road must, in fact, represent a fraction of the ones actually out there.

Figure 2.5.   Author's photograph of Diné College, with sheep grazing on grounds.

I've seen lots of hand painted "Sheep 4 Sale" signs, and the trading post bulletin boards usually have at least one flier selling sheep—about $100 a ewe, more for a ram. I've seen sacks full of raw wool, with their owners waiting for wool prices to rise before bringing them to market. Sheep, as well as cattle and horses, often grazed the greener pastures of Diné College's campus grounds. Trading posts often sell mutton, as does Basha's grocery store in all the major reservation towns. We even had mutton a couple of times at the cafeteria at Diné College, which was much appreciated by the students. If not cut into pieces for a stew, the meat is usually served fried and still on the bone. In fact, that cafeteria mutton meal was mainly notable for the long, white bones that took up most of the plate. Mutton was served at all three of the ceremonies I attended, and, along with big sacks of Blue Bird Flour, was a common food gift on such occasions. Just like turkey at Thanksgiving and ham at Christmas, the Navajo eat mutton on ceremonial or other traditional occasions.

The economic changes brought about by the Depression and stock reduction were further accelerated with the post–World War II industrial boom. Even before the war years many Navajos had engaged in seasonal wage labor, but the trend increased both during and after the war. Much of the wage labor was off reservation, both as agricultural and as wartime factory laborers. By the 1950s, thousands of Navajo men were engaged in railroad construction in the western United States, sometimes leaving their communities for four to six months at a time (Kelley and

Whiteley 1989; Russell 1999). Some Navajo men stayed closer to home and worked in the new field of uranium mining to meet the demands of nuclear weapons production, also a product of the war. After the war the demand for workers increased and Navajo began to travel further from the reservation and for longer periods in search of jobs. The figures from one community provide an example: In 1940 wagework was minimal; by 1952 around 50 percent of the families were dependent on cash from wagework (Blanchard 1970:139). Today, traditional economic pursuits account for between 10 to 20 percent of the total economy; the informal arts and crafts economy, wagework, and welfare provide the most important income sources for Navajo families (Russell 1999). Wage labor—the direct conversion of time into money—paved the Navajo path into the modern era.

Prior to the war, the Navajo had been culturally and geographically isolated from mainstream Anglo-American society (Bailey and Bailey 1986). Despite the patriotic and pivotal role that Navajos[3] played in World War II, most veterans returned to the reservation and reentered their traditional lives. Indeed, the immediate postwar generation of Navajo continued to lead their lives much as their post–Bosque Redondo ancestors had done. Far-reaching postwar economic changes, however, were to permanently alter Navajo life. Prior to 1950, only four paved roads crossed the reservation and in large part were built to meet the needs of surrounding Anglo communities. The postwar industrial boom required that goods move from one location to another with ease, precipitating an increase in road construction. Once roads arrived the Navajo's horse-drawn wagon gave way to the automobile. A trip to the trading post that took several days by horse and wagon could now be accomplished in several hours. The increased ease of transportation, however, meant that gasoline had to be purchased with cash, underscoring the fact that wage labor had become a necessity. These changes saw a rapid decline in the trading posts themselves—from a peak of 137 on-reservation trading posts in 1960, to only 100 in 1970, a 27 percent drop in ten years (Bailey and Bailey 1986). Today, only a dozen or so posts still actively buy Navajo crafts—the rest have either been converted into convenience stores,[4] lay in ruins, or have been demolished.

Wilkinson's Trading Post at Tsaile, home of Diné College, is an odd and eclectic place to shop. Everyone calls Wilkinson's a trading post, although the casual Anglo observer would probably just call it a quick stop convenience store. Many of today's trading posts sit on the site of an older, now demolished post. Others are still in the same building, but with poorly attached recent additions sagging off the original sandstone structures. They have ATM machines, video rentals, small post office boxes, pay phones, and microwave popcorn hanging next to bright skeins of yarn and blue enamel coffeepots imported from Mexico. A small Laundromat may be somewhere in the back. Cedar cradleboards hang in the front window. Small meat departments sell fresh mutton wrapped in wax paper. Hand-woven baskets and hides used in traditional Navajo

Figure 2.6.   Author's photograph of current Old Red Lake Trading Post.

ceremonies may be sold right next to newspapers from Gallup or Flagstaff. One sure thing to be found in every trading post is the inevitable mound of white cotton Blue Bird Flour sacks, the only acceptable flour for making fry bread. In the hot, lazy days of summer people sit around on the old wooden benches that line the shady front porches like the one at Wilkinson's. Reservation trading posts, whether new or old, have not lost their social function.

Increased participation in wage labor, stemming largely from Anglo employ-ment sources, also meant a need to learn English. A surge in school attendance re-sulted—largely through the Bureau of Indian Affairs (BIA) boarding schools—and the number of Navajos who could speak English skyrocketed. Navajos began spending more time in the growing Anglo border towns. These towns were often railroad towns, their rapid growth also directly related to the postwar industrial boom. Missionaries flooded the reservation, promoting a variety of Christian be-liefs. Many Navajo began to leave behind the traditional rural, livestock-oriented lifestyle, moving into the small communities that had sprung up around major trading posts or into the border towns to find work. Coming in relatively quick succession, the Depression, stock reduction, and an increase in wage labor all served to bring Anglo values further and further into the once exclusive domain of Navajo culture.

The shift to wage labor brought with it important kinship changes. Since it was the Navajo man who generally worked for wages during this period, the tra-ditional economic importance of female labor was reduced, as that of the male ex-panded. When land allotments were given to individuals or heads of household,

it was in the male's name. Despite the matrilineal descent system, the Anglo sur-
names as given in schools began to be passed down through the father. Many
newly married couples, following Anglo tradition, came to form new, separate
households, rather than traditional matrilocal postmarital pattern. Thus, the
adoption of a wage-oriented market economy also meant the adoption of western
marriage and residence patterns, causing changes in the matrilineal focus of
Navajo society (Blanchard 1970: 79–80).

Education, Language, and Culture

The boarding schools run by the BIA long served as perhaps the primary means
of instilling Anglo values into Navajo children (Emerson 1983; Prucha 1979).
Since the Navajo were—and mostly still are—dispersed over the landscape, attending school in an era of poor transportation almost always meant living at a
boarding school. It was not uncommon for years to go by without a child going
home to see his or her family. In the Treaty of 1868, the Navajo agreed to send
their children to the white man's schools. Initially, some Navajo refused to deliver
their children to school, oftentimes even hiding them from the authorities (Johnson 1973; Lockyard 1995). Other Navajo, however, abided by the Treaty and sent
their children, particularly after participation in wage labor made it clear to the
Navajo that success now meant learning English.

In the boarding schools, instead of being taught their own history as passed
down in the creation stories, the children learned the history written by and about
the Anglo-Americans. Rather than emphasizing the morals and values important
to their own culture, such as the importance of Spider Woman in Navajo culture,
the schools taught Western values with their pronounced emphasis on the individual rather than the group. Furthermore, Navajo children were educated not in
their native tongue but in English. For the student who was caught speaking the
Navajo language, the punishment was often quick and severe. Many of the schools
offered harsh conditions, and students commonly remember having their culturally appropriate long hair cut, randomly being given English names, having to
march in formation, polish the floors, and go to bed hungry.

*On my visit to her home, Karen showed me around Tuba City, including the old, thick-
walled red sandstone buildings of the BIA boarding school. Although most of her school years
were spent at a BIA boarding school in Utah, she had attended the Tuba City school for a
while. The school, built in the 1930s, was still run as a boarding school by the BIA, although students who lived locally attended as day students, returning home in the afternoon.*

*As we walked around the grounds, Karen pointed out the different buildings. There was the
main classroom building, the girls' and boys' dormitories, and various administration buildings.
All the buildings were tall and towering with imposing architecture, certainly dwarfing the small*

hogans the children called home. Despite the sturdy stone foundations, the buildings were clearly in desperate need of repair, particularly the interiors. Many buildings were completely abandoned, with boarded-up windows and rotting roofs. A groundskeeper let us into one of the buildings, telling us it was now the student union. Two old pool tables stood to one side, with plastic stained glass lights hanging above them. A small snack bar—topped with yellowing, boomerang-designed Formica—offered a very limited menu. A number of tables and chairs—mismatched and obviously scavenged from a variety of uncertain locations—served as seating for the students. The floor sported a lime green carpet, stained and worn thin from well-established, long-term walking routes. Paint was peeling off the walls and several windows had long cracks. The whole room had a musty smell. I later read in the American Indian Report (2000,10) that the BIA's 2001 budget has earmarked money to tear down the old boarding school at Tuba City and replace it with a new one. Although the buildings are beautiful and magnificent historic structures, it would take more money to renovate them to modern standards than it would to tear them down and begin from scratch.

Although some children still attend BIA boarding schools, most are now taken to and from their public, state-run day schools in big yellow school buses that travel the dirt roads far into the rural areas. Karen's seven-year-old daughter, Audrey, attends the public elementary school at Tsaile. When we went to get her out early from school one day, she was in the middle of her Navajo Culture class. Audrey and the other second graders were busily constructing little hogans out of Popsicle sticks and painting them brown. Cotton ball sheep with toothpick legs wandered nearby. Audrey can count to ten in Navajo, and knows quite a bit of vocabulary, but she is far from fluent. Such is the case with many Navajo youth today. Their par-

Figure 2.7.   Author's photograph of elementary school Navajo culture exhibit at Shiprock Fair.

*ents most likely attended BIA boarding schools and learned English, thus preparing them-
selves for employment in the Anglo-dominated workforce. Many of these completely bilingual
parents, however, for a variety of reasons, have not taught their children much Navajo. Tele-
vision—often a universal babysitter in cultures that have it—has greatly accelerated the already quick pace of Navajo language loss.*

In the 1970s, a number of tribally run bilingual and bicultural programs were
established at the elementary, secondary, and post-secondary levels (Emerson
1983). Navajo Community College (now Diné College at Tsaile, Arizona) was
founded in 1968 and offers a number of two-year associates degrees. Just over
four hundred students, mostly Navajo, attend Diné College, either at its main
branch or at its many extended campuses. The college attempts to teach both traditional Navajo and Western beliefs and skills (Weiger 1998). All Diné College
students are required to take nine hours of Navajo study, including culture, language, and history.

In addition to these bilingual and bicultural educational programs, an attempt
is also being made at Navajo literacy. Navajo language has been passed on—un-
written—for many generations. Thus, until recently, Navajo language has been exclusively an oral language. In the late 1800s, Franciscan missionaries started turn-
ing Navajo into a written language by using the English alphabet and adding
linguistic symbols for sounds that do not exist in English. As in many cultures
worldwide, bibles are a common first book to have printed in the newly written
language, and Navajo is no exception. However, very few fluent Navajo speakers
can actually read Navajo, even though billboards and various tribal program slo-
gans are written in Navajo with the hope that it will catch on. Indeed, some young
people today find themselves in the strange position of being able to read Navajo
but not really speak it.

Various tribal programs actively promote Navajo culture, of which bilingual
and bicultural school programs are both examples. The Navajo Nation Museum
in Window Rock regularly features educational programs designed for Navajo.
The tribally sponsored Navajo Nation Fairs are another example of traditional
Navajo culture being actively encouraged, and open for all to appreciate. Indeed,
the Shiprock Fair even sponsors a public Yei-bi-chei ceremony as a means of educating both Navajo and non-Navajo alike about traditional ceremonial practice.
Usually such nine-night ceremonies are very expensive—even as much as several
thousand dollars, as such a huge outlay of time and materials is required of the
medicine man. Each year the patient at the Shiprock Fair—usually an individual
of limited economic means—receives the public ceremony for free, paid for by the
tribe. Indeed, the very public Shiprock Yei-bi-chei in early October has come to
mark the close of summertime with ceremonies such as the Enemyway, and the
start of wintertime ceremonies, such as the Yei-bi-chei.

One thing I noticed right away about being on the Navajo Reservation was the number of fairs. There is a Central Navajo Nation Fair in Chinle, a Southwestern Navajo Nation Fair in Dilkon, a Western Navajo Nation Fair in Tuba City, the Shiprock Fair in Shiprock, and the Annual Navajo Nation Fair in Window Rock, as well as various other smaller fairs and festivals. Although I suppose the fairs are regional so that local people can attend, people from all over the reservation go to many if not all of the major fairs. In addition to Midway rides, games of chance to win a giant pink teddy bear, rodeos, and Powwows, these fairs also sponsor Navajo cultural events such as the Navajo Song and Dance event, and a fry bread contest.

When I learned there was a non-Indian category in the fry bread contest, I really wanted to enter. I thought it would be great fun to try my hand at mixing the dough, shaping the bread, heating the iron skillet over the wood fire, and quickly flopping in the round, flat, raw dough before it splattered too much hot grease all over my arms. After the bread fries to a light brown and has cooled a bit, a group of very serious judges sample each persons' fry bread before it is cut up and distributed to the onlookers packed on bleachers. There were pretty decent prizes, too—I had my eye on a hand-made, full-length apron with the unmistakable bluebird emblem of the famous Blue Bird Flour sack sewn into the chest section.

Unfortunately, by the time Karen and I got around to having a fry bread-making evening, fair season had ended. Nevertheless, I did learn how to make fry bread:

Figure 2.8.   Laura Gilpin, *Making Fry Bread at Blessingway, Crownpoint,* color transparency, © 1979, Amon Carter Museum, Forth Worth, Texas, bequest of the artist.

Mix 1 Tablespoon each of baking powder and salt with 3 or 4 cups of Blue Bird Flour. Gradually add warm water until the dough sticks together but is not too dry. Knead briefly, and place in a covered Tupperware bowl to set for 15 minutes. Heat lard or cooking oil in a skillet until very hot, and press a palm full of dough into a round, flat (⅛ inch) shape about eight inches across. Don't worry too much about holes. Place dough into hot oil and turn constantly until crisp and golden brown—about 1 minute. Always turn dough in a clockwise direction, never counter-clockwise. Remove bread, let cool about 5 minutes on paper towels. Serve with mutton stew. Enjoy!

Even though this recipe may sound straightforward, I came to learn that fry bread actually varies a lot, and that good, fresh, warm fry bread is something truly exquisite. Navajo women rightly take great pride in making good fry bread. I guess I'll just have to be content with imagining owning that wonderful Blue Bird Flour apron until I can perfect my fry bread skills, get back to Navajoland, and enter that fry bread contest.

Current Political Structure

Before European contact, local Navajo headmen led their small local groups. The Spanish appointed Navajo tribal leaders for them, or at least they tried to, as Americans continued the practice of appointing tribal leaders for them. The first Tribal Council was appointed in the 1920s by the BIA. The formation of the Council was not an exercise in democratization. Rather, Council formation was linked to the discovery of oil on the reservation (Shepardson 1983; Wilkins 1999). The rapidly industrializing United States needed oil, and private companies were more than willing to produce it at a high profit.

Since reservation land is held in trust by the federal government for Indians, the government—through the BIA—has oversight concerning the land and all that occurs on it. Oil companies wishing to drill on the reservation had to obtain a federal permit to do so, and the BIA created the Navajo Tribal Council in an effort to facilitate this process in a manner that, at least on the surface, appeared to honor tribal sovereignty. The Council was appointed simply to approve oil leases, not to actually govern the tribe and look out for Navajo resources. Although originally intended as a "rubber stamp" governing body, many of the appointed Council members were uncooperative from the beginning and refused to sign some oil leases, even though the royalties went to the tribe. Overall, such long-standing, paternalistic behavior has produced a general distrust of the motives of the BIA (Oswalt and Neely 1998). Unfortunately, even though the Indian employees currently overwhelmingly dominate the BIA, its personality and behavior has not greatly changed.

It was not until 1938 that the Navajo saw their first, popularly elected leader, J. C. Morgan, in the newly created position of Tribal Chairman (Shepardson

1983; Wilkins 1999). Ironically, Mr. Morgan, a Navajo from Crownpoint, New Mexico, was elected under election and governance rules laid out by the BIA. To this day, Navajo tribal government operates under the 1938 BIA Rules. Even though the majority of other Indian tribes have now written their own tribal constitutions and have taken those constitutions to their members for approval and thus made them legitimate, the Navajo have never done so. Although various drafts of a Navajo constitution have been written over the years, none has ever been taken before tribal members for a vote.

Indeed, it was the problems in the original 1938 BIA Rules that allowed Tribal Chairman Peter MacDonald, a long-serving and influential leader,[5] to accumulate great power in the executive branch (also see Iverson 1983). By the late 1980s, his misuse of power had gotten out of hand with the purchase of Big Boquillas Ranch.

I've heard so many jokes about golf balls since I've been here that I finally had to ask. Even though I didn't get the jokes, I laughed as if I did, but now I simply want to know: What's up with the golf balls? As it turns out, golf balls were an essential element of the charges against Peter MacDonald about misuse of tribal funds in the late 1980s.

Mr. MacDonald, then Tribal Chairman, went in with other non-Navajo people to purchase Big Boquillas Ranch as private, non-trust land for the tribe. The 491,000-acre ranch—prime grazing land near Flagstaff—underwent two sales in the course of about ten seconds, netting a $10 million profit for MacDonald and his co-conspirators. Since it would be suspicious if several million dollars suddenly appeared in the Navajo Tribal Chairman's personal bank account, he made arrangements to call one of his partners-in-crime and ask that a certain amount of "golf balls" be sent. One golf ball equaled $5,000, so a delivery of three golf balls added up to $15,000. Once authorities became suspicious, MacDonald's accomplice double-crossed him, even tape recording their conversations. MacDonald was thrown out of the chairmanship and chaos spread through the tribe. MacDonald's followers rioted in the streets of Window Rock; two Navajos died in the riots.

MacDonald was convicted of numerous counts of bribery, fraud, racketeering, extortion, conspiracy, and of instigating a riot. He was sentenced to fourteen years in federal prison. Sitting in federal prison in Texas in poor health, on January 20, 2001, outgoing President Clinton commuted his sentence to time served, taking five years off his prison time.[6] MacDonald's personal profit was returned to tribal coffers. The ranch is now private property—not federal trust land—of the Navajo tribe. The ranch is currently being leased to non-Indian cattle ranchers and the yearly lease fees go into tribal accounts. The Navajo and other tribes now own a number of tracts of private property, sometimes quite distant from their reservation land. Clearly, many Indian tribes are trying to position themselves for the future.

Due to these embarrassing events, the Tribal Council made long overdue amendments to the 1938 Rules. These 1989 amendments made many important changes: a better system of checks and balances was created; the power of the executive branch was curbed by better distributing power among the three branches; and clear and unambiguous ethics rules were created. Since the 1989 amendments, the head of the executive branch has been called the Tribal President, rather than Tribal Chairman. This name change reflects the fact that current Navajo political structure more closely parallels that of the federal government, even though the Navajo legislative branch has only one chamber (the Tribal Council) rather than two (a House and Senate). Currently, eighty-eight Council Members, each elected for four-year terms with no term limits, sit on the Tribal Council. The Council chambers are in a beautiful old red sandstone Works Progress Administration (WPA) building in Window Rock, not far from the natural rock window that gives the tribal capitol its name.

The smallest political units on the reservation are chapters. The first chapter, Leupp, was created in 1927 by a BIA agent as an extension of grazing units (Shepardson 1983). The idea caught on quickly, and by 1933 there were over 100 chapters. Elected officials run the chapters and hold monthly meetings for all residents. Each chapter has a chapter house with offices, public meeting space, and sometimes a hogan-shaped senior citizen center nearby. Chapters are represented on the Tribal Council based on relative population. Thus, the eighty-eight Council Members represent the 110 chapters, with some sparsely populated chapters sharing a representative and heavily populated chapters having more than one representative. Since 1998 with the passage of the Local Governance Act—an effort to decentralize the tribal government in Window Rock—chapters can follow certain procedures to gain more autonomy. To date, only one chapter—Shonto—has followed these procedures (Navajo Nation Government, Office of Navajo Nation Government Development).

In 1969 the Navajo Tribal Council made a symbolically and conceptually important declaration (Iverson 1983; Wilkins 1999). Prior to this date the Navajo tribal government had officially been called "The Navajo Tribe." By Council declaration they changed their official name to "The Navajo Nation." The term "Nation" denotes a higher degree of self-determination, both over the land within their reservation boundaries and over its members. The adoption and use of the term Nation also underscores the direct government to government (nation to nation) relationship with the federal government.

Thus, it becomes clear that the Navajo, as well as other Indian people, are different than other minorities in the United States. Federally recognized tribes have a legally defined land base and by law are entitled to certain benefits, such as health and education. Enrolled tribal members have triple citizenship: American citizenship, state citizenship depending on residence, and Navajo citizenship. They vote in elections for three major offices that have the power to influence their lives greatly. From traditional, small-scale headmen, through appointed "chiefs," appointed and later elected Tribal Chairmen, and now elected Tribal Presidents, Navajo political structure[7] has seen radical changes through the years.

Navajo Religion

In many ways, Navajo religion is as much about medicine as it is religion. So interconnected are the two that neither religion nor medicine would exist without the other. In mainstream Anglo society religion and medicine are distinct endeavors with minimal overlap. Navajo healing is holistic in that it conceives of an individual as much more than a physical body (Downs 1984; Griffin-Pierce 1992; Wyman 1983). Good health is not an accident, but rather is the result of balance within the individual. Likewise, illness is the result of a lack of balance within the individual. Healing involves the intervention by a medicine man to restore balance through the proper performance of ceremony. Ceremony is meant to focus and concentrate supernatural power and then apply it to restore balance and harmony in the individual, and thus health.

When illness is present, Western medicine primarily treats the body. While in traditional Navajo philosophy the body is also treated, it is only one of four realms that must be considered when an individual is ill. A second realm to be taken into account is the mental realm—an individual's state of mind, whether angry, sad, or bitter, for example. The third realm to be considered is spirituality as expressed through the individual's relationship with the supernatural world. Finally, the fourth realm where illness can originate centers on an individual's relationship to the environment.

Illness results when one or more realms are out of balance. But, how does a realm become unbalanced? Traditional Navajo philosophy teaches that one is to do certain things, and not do other things. In the realm of the physical body, one should engage in hard work and not be lazy. Being lazy will bring about a lack of balance in the physical body. In the mental realm, one is taught to have a positive outlook toward life. If one allows oneself to become bitter and angry, a lack of balance will result in the mental realm. In the spiritual realm, one is taught to perform simple ceremonies to honor Holy People, like Spider Woman. If one does not do these rituals, one's spiritual realm may become unbalanced. In the realm of relationship to the environment one is taught to have respect for nature and not to abuse it. If one clears sagebrush to build a new hogan and does not say the proper prayers to honor the sagebrush, imbalance may result.

Lack of balance in any of these four realms can manifest itself as many kinds of illness. For example, clearing sagebrush without prayer can lead to toothache, a physical body ailment, and just as easily it could lead to sudden outbursts of anger, an ailment of the mental realm. Thus, before a ceremony can be done to restore balance, a diagnosis must first be made to determine the nature of the imbalance, and hence the cause of illness. Navajo diagnosticians use one of two practices, either hand trembling or star and crystal gazing. Hand trembling is where an individual who has hand trembling abilities passes his hands near the patient's body. The manner in which the hand shakes tells the practitioner which realm is out of balance and why. Star or crystal gazing is similar in that the diagnostician looks either at the stars or into a crystal, and the cause of the illness is revealed. Only after the diagnosis has been made can the proper ceremony be determined. Once that ceremony is properly carried out, then balance and health are restored, and the patient becomes healthy again.

As part of my Navajo Holistic Healing class at Diné College, my instructor required us to attend one of the ceremonies he would be conducting that semester. James is a medicine man trained to perform two ceremonies: the Male Shootingway and the Nightway, or Yei-bi-chei. Karen and I decided we would attend his nine-day Yei-bi-chei near Low Mountain. I had already attended the third night of a Yei-bi-chei at the Shiprock Fair's public ceremony, but

Figure 2.9.   Author's Photograph of Yei-bi-chei sign on road.

each night of the ceremony is different. At the Low Mountain Yei-bi-chei we would be at-
tending the final night's activities—the grande finale of the entire ceremony; an all-nighter.

The ceremony was at the patient's home, almost twenty miles down a dirt road. Since it
had been raining for most of the last two weeks, all the dirt roads on the reservation were
quagmires of thick, sloppy mud. As we pushed and dug our way out of the mud for the third
time, it became crystal clear why everyone drove four-wheel drives and why the tribal gov-
ernment is putting so much money into road improvement. We arrived just after nightfall,
mud all over us, hungry and cold, and happy to finally be there. We brought our gifts—a
mutton leg and a ten-pound sack of Blue Bird Flour—into the hogan where the food was
being served. We didn't know anyone, since our instructor was in the ceremonial hogan. Fol-
lowing Karen's lead, I went around and quietly shook everyone's hand, with a low
Yá'át'ééh (hello). We ate potato salad, blood sausage, mutton stew, fry bread, and chocolate
cake. Along with everyone else gearing up for the long night ahead, we drank lots of Arbuckle's
brewed-on-the-wood-stove coffee.

I noticed that our sack of flour was piled on top of about fifty other such sacks, and that
our mutton leg was jammed into the already jam-packed freezer. James later told me that this
family had started preparing for this ceremony two years in advance and that these items,
along with many more, would be redistributed after the ceremony to the many, many people
who had helped. Mostly clan relatives, these individuals were needed to donate both time and
money to pull off such a long and complicated ceremony. Wood had to be hauled and chopped
for all-night bonfires, herbs had to be collected, a brush hogan had to be built for the dancers,
lights had to be strung over the dance plaza, food had to be bought and cooked for hundreds
of guests, and the medicine man had to be paid. Clearly, this was not a ceremony one un-
dertook lightly, or alone. Responsibility to one's clan was unmistakable during such times.

The patient, a man in his late 40s, had been feeling dizzy and having eye problems for a
number of years. He went to see a hand trembler to find out what was wrong. The hand
trembler told the man his problems were the result of seeing a ceremonial sandpainting when
he was not properly initiated, thus offending the Holy People. After seeking a second opin-
ion, the patient and his family decided to undertake this colossal event.[8]

After eating, we walked over to the ceremonial area and entered the huge ceremonial hogan.
The hogan, nearly forty feet across, was made out of logs and had a dirt floor, as all cere-
monial hogans must. Women sat to the north, men to the south, the medicine man sat a lit-
tle to the southwest, and the patient—translated from Navajo as "the person sung over"—
a little to the northwest. The medicine man, assisted by a handful of men, chanted songs while
beating a steady rhythm on an upside down ceremonial basket. Outside, four huge fires
burned the entire night. Every so often a group of dancers would appear. Since this was the
grand finale night, they were all dressed up: leather masks with corn stalk images painted

across the face and eagle feathers sewn upright on the seams; evergreen boughs around their necks and shoulders; bright, shiny, sequin-bedecked kilts with fox pelt tails hanging from their waists. Any exposed skin—and there was a lot of exposed skin for around 30 degrees—was painted with white clay. The dancers shook gourd rattles and chanted in unison. No one made a mistake the entire night—clearly the dancers were quite practiced. The patient, sitting in a lawn chair at the west end of the dance plaza, simply watched. Occasionally, between songs, the medicine man came out and instructed the patient to say and do various things, like sprinkle cornmeal over the dancers, or offer it to the four directions.

The dancers represented—or were—Yé'ii. Yé'ii are supernatural beings—Holy People—that helped create the world. They are unable to speak, but can make sounds, as did the masked dancers in front of the ceremonial hogan. Yé'ii possess great power that can be called upon to restore balance—and thus health and well-being—to individuals.

Karen and I went between the dance plaza and the ceremonial hogan to listen to the chanting and to take the opportunity to sit down and warm up. A Navajo family with an entrepreneurial spirit had converted the back of their rusty old van into a concession stand on wheels. A cardboard sign duct-taped to the back door announced their menu: hamburgers, burritos, and hot chocolate, all cooked over a kerosene stove. Being the only Anglo there—out of around a hundred people—at first I felt painfully conspicuous, but after awhile everyone seemed to simply accept my presence and go about their business. In fact, when we were leaving, several people—the patient included—came up, shook my hand, and thanked me for coming. Our instructor later told me that the patient was feeling much better.

Although both men and women may become medicine men, the great majorities are male, probably due to fears of exposing the unborn to an excessive amount of supernatural power (Wyman 1983). Usually, women who become ceremonial practitioners do so after they have passed their childbearing years. Typically, there are more women diagnosticians than there are actual practitioners of ceremonies. Medicine men and diagnosticians have never been full-time specialists. Rather, prior to the postwar years, they grew crops and raised livestock like everyone else; or, these days, they work for wages, like everyone else. Sandpainting, chanting, drumming, rattling, ritual bathing, dancing, giving blessings, and making offerings are common parts of all ceremonies, all arranged in staggering complexity.

Most medicine men know only one ceremony, or very few, due to the length of time necessary to learn the precise ritual requirements of any given ceremony. This long time requirement has meant that few young Navajo are now interested in becoming a medicine man, even if they still believe that supernatural forces influence healing. As a result of the blending of Navajo tradition with the expectations of modern society, many ceremonies have been shortened and simplified (Downs 1984; Wyman 1983).

Not only have ceremonies been shortened as a result of the time and energy required, but many ceremonies are on their way to extinction; some are already extinct. Prior to European contact, there may have been hundreds of different Navajo ceremonies performed. As western medicine, wage labor, missionaries, BIA and American public school systems, and overall exposure to Anglo ways has increased, the number and variety of Navajo ceremonies have decreased. The most common ceremonies performed today are Blessingway, the Yei-bi-chei, and the Enemyway (also called a Squaw Dance, due to its original association with returning warriors and courtship opportunities on this proud occasion).

During the 1960s the Navajo Medicine Men's Association was founded. The teaching of traditional Navajo religion has since enjoyed a revival, and its practitioners now express their concerns about the inappropriate public display of sacred items and information in many museums throughout the country. In 1977, the Navajo Museum's board of trustees acknowledged the wisdom and authority of the Navajo Medicine Men's Association by voting to repatriate a number of Navajo medicine bundles and other items sacred to the Navajo people. The Navajo Nation now maintains these items at the Ned A. Hatathli Cultural Center Museum at Diné College. Among other activities, the Medicine Men's Association attempts to find young Navajo interested in learning ceremonies, particularly those ceremonies rarely performed today.

The Native American Church[9] (NAC) plays a very important religious role on the Navajo Reservation today. The NAC's origins stem back to the late 1800s with Indian confinement to reservations, particularly in the Plains (Aberle 1983a; Smith and Snake 1996). The Kiowa are often given credit for being the originators of this new, syncretic religion. In 1918 the NAC was officially founded through the work of many tribes, and today claims an intertribal membership of over 250,000, which would constitute the largest of any Native American religious organization.

The NAC has long been active on the Navajo Reservation. Its origins among the Navajo date back to the 1920s, when Utah Navajos began interacting more with members of the neighboring Utes. Since then the religion has spread over the entire Navajo Reservation, particularly in response to the profound changes brought about through stock reduction and the Depression. The Navajo Tribal Council banned the Church in 1940 as a threat to both native Navajo culture and Christian Navajos, but adherents practiced covertly until the council reversed its ban in 1967. Over 700 arrests resulted during this ban (Aberle 1983a, 566). Navajos do not usually practice one religion to the exclusion of others, however, so traditional Navajo religion, Christianity, and NAC meetings, for example, can be freely participated in by the same individual without a sense of contradiction.

Figure 2.10.   Author's photograph of Diné College's Ned Hatathli Building, the college's ceremonial hogan, and stacked teepee poles for Native American Church meetings.

The main intents of the NAC are to heal, bless, or thank. The ideology of the NAC is Pan-Indian, because it emphasizes the unity of all Indians, regardless of tribal origin, and their distinctness from whites. The religion is also nativistic, in that there is an emphasis on ritual details and ritual equipment, and a desire to keep the religion only for Indians. The religion is syncretic, as much of the symbolism is Christian, with the figures of God, Mary, Jesus, and the Heavenly Angels playing central roles in prayer. Peyote (*Lophophora williamsii*), consumed as a sacrament, encourages communication with God and warm feelings to both purify the participants and to channel group and supernatural power for healing. Although other—and particularly some New Age churches—also use Peyote, a nonaddictive, mind-altering substance, the NAC is the only institution legally able to do so.

As midterm exams approached at Diné College, I started hearing about the canvas teepee that would be erected next to the college's ceremonial hogan, itself next to one of the main classroom buildings. There was to be an NAC meeting to pray for good grades. Clearly, it was to be a big event, and lots of students were going. One of my instructors was the Roadman, the equivalent of a medicine man for the NAC. Several of my Navajo instructors, in addition to being medicine men, are also NAC Roadmen. Another instructor told us in class that there were so many Roadmen simply "coming out of the woodwork" these days that the NAC national office was trying to create a certification process for Roadmen. Indeed, a friend took me to visit his uncle, who was a Roadman. He had a dream one night that he should become a Roadman, and the next day he began leading meetings. Translating through his nephew, he told me he donated much of his land to the Church, space that is used for educational and cultural activities for Navajo children, sponsored by the NAC.

At the college, I knew many people involved with the NAC, and I enquired whether I would be welcome at the all-night meeting in the teepee. I was told that only NAC card-carrying members would be admitted, and that to get a card, you had to be Indian. Oh well. Even without attending I could hear the rhythmic, Plains-style drumming from just about anywhere on campus. I figured I'd go check out the teepee from a respectful distance the next morning. But by the time I got out that Saturday morning around eight o'clock, the teepee was already down and no sign remained that a major meeting had just taken place. Apparently taking down the teepee immediately after the meeting is part of the process. I've seen this several times since—a teepee up in a yard one day, and gone the next—the only clue you have that NAC meetings occur is a stack of teepee poles, raised off the ground by a simple metal rack.

I've seen Diné College students pack like sardines into a car, all holding their colorful, fringed, Pendleton wool blankets—a strong symbol of Indian identity as well as being useful for wrapping up against the cold night. They'll pull up back at the College in time for breakfast in the cafeteria, smelling of the wood fire that burned all night long in the teepee. With their eyes propped open with toothpicks, they'll attend their classes and study as best they can. Then they'll go crash. I've also noticed a lot of distrust and outright prejudice by some Navajos toward other Navajos heavily into NAC. One person told me she thinks they're a bunch of space cadets from taking too much peyote. Another person told me they're too political—too into Red Power—and just stir up trouble.

The NAC is a good example of a trend toward Pan-Indianism that first began through BIA boarding schools, which often brought together Indians from many different tribes. The Navajo Reservation has a goodly number of Plains-style sweat lodges—saplings bent together to form a dome, and covered with tarps, carpets, and blankets. I've also seen long strips of colorful cloth—Plains prayer flags—tied to trees. Navajos are active Powwow dancers both on and off the reservation, and I've been told they do Sun Dances on the reservation as well. Clearly, Plains-derived, Pan-Indian culture and religion is strong on the Navajo Reservation.

Participation in a wide variety of religious ceremonies is not generally considered contradictory by Navajos (Aberle 1983a; Bailey and Bailey 1986). Participation in NAC meetings is often understood as attending another kind of Navajo traditional ceremony, or "sing." Mormonism is strong on the reservation, as are a wide variety of Protestant Christian denominations—only Catholicism has not won significant converts among Navajos. Pentecostal tent revivals are not uncommon on the reservation. Again, members of these congregations feel free to participate, and often do, in the ceremonial activities of other faiths ,and may change their religious affiliation numerous times.

Despite and perhaps because of the relatively recent changes to Navajo culture and religion, a kind of quiet renaissance has occurred. Even though Navajos have certainly never been meek in their interaction with the non-Navajo world, they seem to have a new confidence in themselves. They have a clear sense of justice, their rights, and the value of their culture. This confidence centers on accepting and even embracing new technology and change, but with a clear consideration of how that change impacts other, more traditional aspects of life that are of equal importance. Changing Woman, the Twins, and Spider Woman are not figments of their ancestors' imagination, but still play important roles in the lives of modern Navajo today, and particularly so for traditional Navajo. After all, it was Spider Woman's generous gift of life-feathers that made—and continues to make—the Fifth World safe for all the five-fingered Earth Surface People.

Notes
1. Go to "Navajo Rugs of Hubbell Trading Post National Historic Site," Southwest Parks and Monuments Association, at <http://navajorugs.spma.org> to see some Navajo rugs. Due to the increased transportation and communication of the modern era, styles are no longer regionally specific; a Ganado rug, originally confined to the south central area of the reservation, can now be made and sold anywhere.

2. Other livestock were also included in these range estimates. One horse equaled five sheep, and one cow equaled four sheep. Stock reduction brought in a variety of range regulations, including the division of reservation land into grazing districts. Livestock could not be taken across district lines, permits would be issued for grazing, and no one could hold a permit for more than 350 sheep units.

3. Using the Navajo language to create a military code that the Japanese never cracked, the Navajo Code Talkers basically won the war in the Pacific. The Code Talkers are much celebrated on the reservation, where they frequently appear in parades wearing their bright yellow uniform shirts and turquoise necklaces, as onlookers stand and cheer. A Hollywood movie, *Windtalkers*, tells their story, and toymaker Hasbro has recently introduced the Navajo Code Talker G.I. Joe, the company's first doll to speak a Native American language.

4. Tony Hillerman has written many great detective novels set in Navajoland. In order to solve crimes, Navajo police officer Jim Chee needs to rely on understanding his own Navajo culture. Recently, one of Hillerman's novels was made into a movie produced by Robert Redford—the *Dark Wind*. The movie is set on the Navajo Reservation, and the Old Red Lake Trading Post makes an appearance. Watch for the wall made out of Arbuckle's coffee crates.

5. For a discussion of positive and negative aspects of Peter MacDonald's leadership, see Harvey (1996).

6. "Ex-Navajo leader's sentence commuted," *Arizona Daily Star*, January 1, 2001.

7. See <www.navajo.org> for more information on the Navajo Nation government and links to a variety of tribal programs.

8. For other and fuller descriptions of a Yei-bi-chei, see Faris (1990), Matthews (1902), and Waters (1950, 22–40).

9. See <www.csp.org/communities/docs/fikes-nac_history.html> for a longer history of the Native American Church.

Creation and Navajo Sacred Geography   3

OST VISITORS TO THE AMERICAN SOUTHWEST come to see the spectacular, awe-inspiring landscape that stretches for miles in all directions. Each year, tourists from all over the globe stream through by the
thousands to behold the dramatic and astonishing vistas of the Grand Canyon
and Monument Valley. Through Hollywood's Westerns, many of these landscapes are familiar to us even if we have never visited them ourselves. To the indigenous inhabitants of the land, however, these locations are valuable for far
more than their aesthetic qualities. First and foremost, these places hold cultural
and religious value for the Navajo—a kind of sacred geography—that literally
grounds the culture to the land. To the Navajo, these landscapes are the physical
manifestation of events that occurred during the creation of the Navajo people
and of the earth itself.

According to the Navajo creation story, a series of four previous worlds existed underneath the present earth's surface (Gill 1983; Matthews 1902; Zolbrod
1984). Each world saw the progressively more complex creation of new land, new
elements, and new beings. The *Nihookáá' dine'é*, the five-fingered Earth Surface People, emerged into the Fifth World through a hollow reed in the ground. As such,
their creation was an Emergence *from* the earth, much like a corn plant pushes
forth from the earth as it grows, with deep roots stretching back and connecting
it to the memory and power of its origins. Without the presence of these stabi-
lizing roots—the physical places of spiritual connection to their own creation—
traditional Navajo would begin to lose their cultural bearings. Indeed, much of
the psychological trauma during the Bosque Redondo incarceration stemmed
from their physical separation from the land that gave them spiritual birth. The
landforms themselves are the visible, highly charged, ever-present personal and
cultural reference points that serve to make daily life rich and meaningful. Thus,

traditional Navajo religion is land-based, in that specific locations embody various kinds of supernatural power.

As physical manifestations of creation era events, these landforms are considered too sacred for recreational and casual resource extraction. Any approach on them requires specific prayer, song, and offering rituals. In addition, trained medicine men must perform such rituals, and must visit these sacred locations on a regular basis to ensure that illness and misfortune do not befall the Earth Surface People. Perhaps even more important, if a sacred place is desecrated, the place itself may lose its beneficent power, and the desecration may even release dangerous power, thus harming all Navajo, and indeed, all of humanity (Jett 1993).

In Navajo philosophy, nothing proceeds on its own; no event or happening is random or coincidental. Rather, all of life flows according to supernatural intervention—with either favorable or unfavorable results—that can be influenced by human ritual action. The Navajo universe is alive with sentient, supernatural beings—the Holy People—that take an active interest in the activities of humans, and pay particular attention to the rituals they perform. These beings will help or punish as they see fit. For example, in addition to the tremendous help already given by Spider Woman, it is said she also saved a young Navajo hunter who was being chased by an enemy tribesman. She performed this miracle by lowering a section of her silken web cord, so that he could climb up her straight-sided home—Spider Rock—to safety (Skinner 1896).

Thus, everyday Navajo life is thickly embedded with ritual. Even apparently mundane activities like weeding the garden must be done with the proper rituals, as incorrectly weeding a garden can anger the supernatural forces that protect the garden, bringing crop failure to you and your family. This is a great risk indeed, and rather than tempt fate, most traditional Navajo people will unfailingly learn and perform the correct rituals necessary to keep the supernatural beings happy. Thus, the relationship is a mutual one—humans perform proper ritual to honor the supernatural, and the supernatural takes care of the humans. All ritual, if performed correctly, must work. If the ritual does not work, it is because it was performed incorrectly. Without the aid of ritual, life in this world can appear threatening and unpredictable, and it is difficult for human beings to live in a constant state of psychological danger.

In light of the risks involved, the care and protection of many of these natural landscape features is no trifling matter for traditional Navajo, as their own well-being hangs in the balance. The more important the creation era event, the more powerful the location. As these locations are imbued with supernatural power, they are ideal places for ritual equipment to be renewed, medicinal plants to be gathered, and sanctified soil and water to be collected (Jett 1995). Interruptions in these activities—be they coal mining, a humming microwave tower on a peak, or tourists with cameras—may render the rituals themselves ineffective, and at the very least, disagreeable to perform.

These sacred locations and beings fall under the general headings of mountains, rock formations, earth and sky, rivers and streams, plants, and animals. Anasazi archaeological sites and the locations of particular ceremonies are also important places, even though there may be no visible land forms that appear unique. The following information is summarized in large part from Linford (2000) and McPherson (1992). Gulliford (2000) discusses other kinds of sacred locations for a variety of American cultures.

The Four Sacred Mountains and Other Rock Formations

For the Navajo, life is special within the space created by the Four Sacred Mountains.[1] These mountains are known today as Blanca Peak, Mt. Taylor, the San Francisco Peaks, and Hesperus Peak. The First Man and First Woman created the four sacred mountains with soil[2] brought from the lower worlds into the current earth's surface world. Many medicine men carry soil from these four mountains in their medicine bundles. These mountains serve as the principal source of Navajo strength and prosperity. Each mountain is associated with a cardinal direction, a color, and with certain Holy People from the creation era—the inner forms of the mountains.

Although these mountains do not actually correspond to the four cardinal directions, they nevertheless create a space that is of particular significance to the Navajo. These mountains are envisioned as representing the four cornerposts that form the support structure for a hogan (Kelley and Francis 1994). Thus, the space inside the mountains is literally the home of the Navajo people. Only within the space created by these mountains—the symbolic Navajo homeland—can curing rituals work. Today, not one of these mountains is on the Navajo Reservation, thus none of the primary support poles of the Navajo cultural hogan are under direct Navajo control.

Beginning in the east, the location of the rising sun, is Blanca Peak, or *Sisnaajinii* (Descending Black Belt or Mountain), probably so named due to its highly visible timberline. The Navajo also refer to as White Shell Mountain, because First Man and First Woman decorated this first-created mountain with white shell. Thus, white—the color of dawn—is associated with Blanca Peak. Talking God, Rock Crystal Boy, and Rock Crystal Girl are the inner forms associated with the mountain. Today, Blanca Peak sits in the state of Colorado, as a part of the Rio Grande National Forest, administered by the U.S. Forest Service.

Following the sun's passage in the sky, to the south sits Mount Taylor, or *Tsoodził*, (Tongue Mountain). First Man decorated this mountain with turquoise,

Figure 3.1.   Laura Gilpin, *Navaho Sacred Mountain of the East,* gelatin silver print, 1953, ©
1979, Amon Carter Museum, Fort Worth, Texas, gift of the artist.

making blue—the color of the midday sky—associated with Mount Taylor, also
known as Turquoise Mountain. Black God, Turquoise Boy, and Turquoise Girl are
the immortals connected with Mount Taylor. When the Twins killed Yé'iitsoh, his
coagulated blood poured over the land around Mt. Taylor. Today, this area is
known as the Grants Lava Flow, El Malpais, and is administered by the National

Figure 3.2.   Laura Gilpin, *Tsoodził, Sacred Mountain of the South*, gelatin silver print, Mar. 11, 1957, © 1979, Amon Carter Museum, Fort Worth, Texas, bequest of the artist.

Park Service and the Bureau of Land Management. Today, Mount Taylor is in New Mexico, a part of the Cibola National Forest.

The San Francisco Peaks, or *Dook'o'oosłííd* (Never Thaws on Top), is the sacred mountain of the west, also known as Abalone Shell Mountain. Yellow—the color of the setting sun—as well as Abalone Girl, White Corn Boy, and White Corn

Figure 3.3.   Laura Gilpin, *Doko'oosliid, Sacred Mountain of the West,* gelatin silver print, 1957, © 1979, Amon Carter Museum, Fort Worth, Texas, bequest of the artist.

Girl are linked with the Peaks. Part of Arizona's Coconino National Forest, the Peaks have seen the most economic development of all the four sacred Navajo mountains, including a ski resort and the industrial-scale mining of volcanic pumice to make stonewashed jeans.

Today the northern mountain is called Hesperus Peak, or *Dibé Ntsaa* (Big Sheep Mountain). First Man adorned this mountain with jet, making black the

Figure 3.4.   Laura Gilpin, *Dibéentsaaa, Sacred Mountain of the North*, gelatin silver print, Nov. 26, 1963, © 1979, Amon Carter Museum, Fort Worth, Texas, bequest of the artist.

color associated with the mountain, as well as the color of the night sky. Monster Slayer, Pollen Boy, and Grasshopper Girl are the immortals that are associated with Hesperus Peak. Today, the mountain is part of the San Juan National Forest in Colorado.

The following quote is from medicine man Slim Curly's version of Blessing-way (Wyman 1970, 325–26). Blessingway was the first ceremony taught to the

Earth Surface People by the Holy People, and thus serves as the foundation for all
other Navajo ceremonies. The sacred mountains are called by name, and are
imbedded within repetitive ritual singing. Indeed, the "ritual repetition of the descriptive names of these places provides for the Navajo a mental map of their domain and reaffirms their possession thereof" (Jett 1993, 30). First Man taught
ritual singing to the Navajo when he gave them permission to climb the four sacred mountains. A song such as this would be sung (in Navajo) in a hogan during
a Blessingway ceremony by a medicine man.

> 'Ai ne ya . . . at dawn I go about, ni yo o.
> Talking God, usually I am!
> Now I have ascended Blanca Peak, I have ascended Chief Mountain.
> I have ascended long life, I have ascended happiness.
> Before me it is blessed where I go about, behind me it is blessed where
>   I go about, as that I continue to go about, at dawn I go about, ni
>   yo o.
>
> Those Holy People from the east left for the east in a group.
>
> At dawn I go about, as that I go about, ni yo o.
> Calling God, usually I am!
> I have ascended Mount Taylor, I have ascended Chief Mountain.
> I have ascended long life, I have ascended happiness.
> Before me it is blessed where I go about, behind me it is blessed where
>   I go about, as that I continue to go about, at dawn I go about, ni
>   yo o.
>
> Then those Holy People from the south also left in a group for the
>   south.
>
> At dawn I go about, Talking God usually I am!
> I have ascended San Francisco Peak, I have ascended Chief Mountain.
> I have ascended long life, I have ascended happiness.
> Before me it is blessed where I go about, behind me it is blessed where I
>   go about, as that I continue to go about, at dawn I go about, ni yo o.
>
> Those Holy People from the west also left in a group for the west.
>
> At dawn I go about, Calling God usually I am!
> I have ascended Hesperus Peak, I have ascended Chief Mountain.
> I have ascended long life, I have ascended happiness.
> Before me it is blessed where I go about, behind me it is blessed where I
>   go about, as that I continue to go about, at dawn I go about, ni yo o.

The Holy People from the north had also left for the north; none of the groups were left. . . .

Although these four mountains are the most sacred, and together form the four support posts to the hogan of the Navajo universe, other mountains are also of particular importance to the Navajo. Gobernador Knob, Huerfano Mesa, and Hosta Butte are all in Dinétah, the birthplace of early Navajo culture. First Man and First Woman made their home on Huerfano Mesa, and the infant Changing Woman was born on Gobernador Knob. Hosta Butte is the home of Mirage Stone Boy and Mirage Stone Girl. In the physical world, male and female mirage stones form the core of a talking prayer stick, an essential piece of ceremonial paraphernalia for a medicine man. The use of talking prayer sticks assure that the Holy People will hear the prayers being said in their honor. As with the four sacred mountains, Gobernador Knob, Huerfano Mesa, and Hosta Butte are not on the Navajo Reservation. Rather, the Bureau of Land Management is the federal agency with jurisdiction over these mountains.

Navajo Mountain (Earth Woman or Head of the Earth) is on the Navajo Reservation, in the state of Utah. Navajo Mountain is said to be the head of a woman, Black Mesa her body, Tuba Butte and Agathla Peak are her breasts, Comb Ridge and a raised area near Marsh Pass are her arms, and Balakai Mesa are her feet (Linford 2000). The vast size of this woman reveals the different scales that are included in the conceptualization of land as the physical manifestation of the sacred.

In addition to mountains, unusual rock formations are often associated with supernatural beings or events that occurred during Creation. Buttes, spires, abrupt mesas or cliff faces, unusual wind-eroded features or oddly shaped boulders may have a connection with creation era beings. By tying specific geographical locations to mythological events, those events are made real and provide both cultural meaning and personal orientation for life. Power far greater than the human realm can be accessed through visiting these places. The power can only be attained, however, by performing rituals specific to that place, which have been passed down through many generations of medicine men. Such rituals usually entail prayers, chanted songs, and offerings of plants, such as sage, and minerals, such as turquoise or jet, or cornmeal and corn pollen. This power affords protection from danger as well as good fortune, and hence is extremely valuable.

Earth and Sky

The earth is female, the sky is male, and they join to create unity. The offspring of Mother Earth (Changing Woman) and Father Sun are the Twins—Monster

Slayer and Born for Water—who made the land inhabitable for humans by killing the Monsters that populated the earth. Such male and female dualism can also be seen in the above listing of supernatural beings associated with the four sacred mountains. By necessity, each mountain contains both female and male elements, as does the larger world—earth and sky.

Rituals need to be performed during both lunar and solar eclipses, to ensure that the celestial object recovers to its proper form. A variety of clouds are classified according to their shape and color. Male clouds are dark and heavy, while female clouds are light and puffy. Rain is also characterized according to this duality; female rain is a light, gentle, soaking rain, while male rain arrives in torrential downpours. Objects or places struck by lightning are considered to have great supernatural power, and must be approached carefully. People gathering firewood are careful not to collect wood from trees that have been struck by lightning; rather, such wood is sometimes collected by medicine men due precisely to its power association. Wind has specific locations where it resides, often at places where the wind howls or has carved out holes in the sandstone.

For a horticultural society, rain is closely equated with life, and as such, much ritual surrounds it. Natural springs, water seeps, river junctions, water basins, and human-made water bowls placed in Anasazi sites are all locations where rain rituals are performed. Because many of the rituals associated with these places are no longer performed, there is not as much rain as there once was. Contrary to the western notion that humans are meant to dominate nature, quite the opposite is true in Navajo belief; humans are meant to be interactive with nature, and to be humble in the presence of the Holy People. In an environment where the presence or absence of rain may mean feast or famine, to risk angering the supernatural forces that bring the rain is foolhardy indeed.

In addition to healing the sick, some medicine men are said to be able to influence the weather, as controlled by the sky spirits. Indeed, John Ford, who directed many Hollywood movies[3] on location in Monument Valley, paid a local medicine man to provide good weather for their crews. Apparently, Mr. Ford was not disappointed in the results.

Rivers and Streams

As with the four mountains that create the boundaries of the traditional Navajo universe, four rivers also form important boundaries. The area within the San Juan, the Colorado, the Rio Grande, and the Little Colorado Rivers creates a special place for the Navajo. In the old days, people only crossed the rivers for hunting or for warfare, both pursuits that involved killing, death, and danger. Purification rituals would be performed upon their return. Indeed, yet another psychological trauma for the Navajo during their Bosque Redondo incarceration was that they had crossed these rivers without the proper preparatory protection. More recently, a Navajo man whose son went to Vietnam is known to have prayed at the confluence of Mancos Creek and the San Juan River for his son's safe return, quite possibly a longstanding and well-known traditional location for warriors to pray for success in battle.

Hunting that occurred across these rivers had specific rituals associated with it. For example, a deer taken across the river must always have its feet and hide removed before transport back into Navajo territory. Even the language spoken by travelers in their journey across the river is different than the language they speak when they are within their own land. Across the river, language is oriented to death and violence, whereas the hunters and warriors were not allowed to speak of such things in their own land.

In the old days, when people needed to cross one of these rivers, they sprinkled corn pollen and said specific prayers. Today, many Navajo people live outside of this region and indeed the reservation extends in some cases well beyond these rivers. Navajo cross these rivers frequently today. The younger Navajo no longer say the prayers or sprinkle the corn pollen, if they even consider the significance of crossing the rivers at all. Many traditional Navajo believe that the rivers have become polluted due to this lack of concern for ritual.

Plants and Animals

Corn is probably the plant most central to Navajo life. As such, much ritual surrounds activities like the selection and preparation of the cornfield, planting, tending, and harvesting. Cornmeal and corn pollen are featured prominently in many Navajo ceremonies. First Man and First Woman were formed from ears of white and yellow corn respectively. This philosophy means that white corn and its pollen and meal are associated with men, and yellow corn and its pollen and meal are associated with women. White corn belongs to the east, and yellow corn belongs to the west, thus linking and balancing the two sexes with these cardinal directions as well.

The collection, preparation, and use of medicinal plants are also steeped in ritual designed to increase the healing power of the plant, at the discretion of the plant spirits. Wild plants used in healing include yucca, cliffrose, mint, devil's claw, larkspur, and the pitch and burnt cones from ponderosa pine. All have sacred names that are used in ritual, and the medicine man will tell the plant spirits specific details such as who is sick and the nature and location of the pain. Clearly, the use of herbs requires not only a botanical recognition of the plants, but also training in the proper rituals necessary during the searching, collection, and preparation of the plants. In Navajo belief, understanding the physical, medicinal properties of the plants is only a fraction of the knowledge necessary to be a medicine man.

Animals are also important in the Navajo worldview. Animals accompanied humans in their emergence, although they only acquired their current form in the present world. Coyote is well known throughout the western United States, and often appears as a Trickster[4] figure in many Indian mythologies. Navajo oral narrative is no exception, with an abundance of Coyote stories that tell of his mischievous ways. One tale recounts how Coyote and Skunk together capture and kill some prairie dogs to cook for dinner. Being greedy, Coyote challenges Skunk to a race; the winner takes all of the prairie dog meat. Skunk agrees, but then tricks Coyote by hiding in a badger hole and waiting until Coyote passes before the wise Skunk returns to the fire to eat all the meat. These tales serve as lessons in correct behavior; if you do not behave properly, there will be consequences for your actions, just as Coyote is punished for being greedy.

Bear is also an important and powerful supernatural creature for the Navajo. Bears are so powerful, in fact, that even bear tracks are treated with great respect. Since bears possess great healing power, they should never be ridiculed, and are only killed under very specific circumstances, always accompanied by prayers and an explanation for the killing. In its physical manifestation, bears reside in the mountains, and hence feature prominently in ceremonies that involve mountains. Like all other power in the Navajo world, Bear's healing power is reached through prayer and ceremony.

Of the domestic animals, sheep are probably the most important. A person's wealth, in part, is determined by the size of his sheep herd, which represents a large future supply of meat and wool, and in turn symbolizes both food and the ability to generate income. Thus, in many respects, the size and quality of the sheep herd reflects an individual's good standing with the supernatural world. Ritual surrounds such activities as opening the corral in the morning to let the sheep out, leading them to a watering hole, arriving at a specific grazing ground, and beginning the return journey home (Downs 1984).

It is interesting that sheep, introduced by the Spanish, have quickly come to occupy such a central ceremonial role. Likewise, corn only came to the Navajo upon their entry into the Southwest. The prominence of corn-based ritual, like corn itself, was taught to the Navajo by their Pueblo neighbors. Ritual, as a central expression of religion, is conservative by nature. Rappaport (2001) describes ritual as more or less invariant sequences of formal acts and utterances that in general do not change very rapidly. However, the speed of these additions and their incorporation into Navajo belief suggests that in some instances, culture is quite malleable, and can be easily adapted to changing circumstances. Indeed, the rapid incorporation of sheep and corn into Navajo ritual philosophy reflects the speed in which these new items became of central economic importance to the Navajo.

Local Cultural Places

Although land forms are usually considered the most important kind of sacred place to the Navajo (Kelley and Francis 1994, 42), other kinds of locations are also meaningful. Major landforms have meaning at a tribal scale, and symbolize the land and culture of the Navajo as a whole. These places always figure prominently in Navajo origin stories. However, former hogans, burials, ceremonially-related plant and mineral gathering locations, shrines, prayer and offering places, and sweat lodges may be significant to individual Navajos at a more local, family scale. These locations, even though they may be unused today, were places where ceremonies were performed. These places absorbed power generated from the performance of ceremonies that were themselves designed to tap into the power of the Holy People. The longer a place has been used for ceremonial purposes, the more power it has absorbed.

Anasazi Archaeological Sites

Archaeologists believe the Anasazi left the Four Corners region around 1300 A.D. due to a combination of factors. These factors include long-term drought, warfare, overpopulation and nucleation, and religious pulls from the developing kachina cult to the south (see papers in Adler 1996), often leaving dramatic ruins in their wake. This movement involved tens of thousands of people over a relatively short period of time. Numerous household items were left behind, suggesting a quick departure to a distant destination to which carrying bulky or heavy items would have made little sense.

If, as is suggested by oral narrative, the Navajo arrived in the Southwest before 1300 A.D., it is possible that they may have played a role in the departure of the Anasazi (Faris 1990, 17). Regardless what such a role may have been, Navajo oral tradition recounts that the Anasazi were driven from their homes by a whirlwind in supernaturally-derived punishment for abandoning their traditional ways (McPherson 1992; Milne 1995). This belief probably tells us more about the Navajo value system than it does about the Anasazi past. As all cultures seek to make sense of their surroundings, and since Anasazi ruins were so prominent in the Navajo's new territory, it is natural that the Navajo would interpret these sites in a manner consistent with their worldview. Why did these people depart so rapidly? To the Navajo, who arrived in the Southwest relatively recently, the only reasonable explanation for the ruins was that the Anasazi had incurred the wrath of their gods—the supernatural beings that punish and reward according to the

Figure 3.5.   Author's photograph of Anasazi (Ancestral Pueblo) archaeological site at Mesa Verde National Park, Colorado.

proper displays of respect. What could be more disrespectful than to disregard the rituals that the supernatural beings request? The lesson is clear: to avoid the fate of the Anasazi, the Navajo must, without err, carry on the traditional ways that have been handed down through the generations.

Guides for Proper Conduct

All cultures have their own set of expected behaviors, many of which are based in religion. For Christianity, expected behavior is expressed in the Ten Commandments and in the Bible. For Muslims, the Koran furnishes this guidance. Adherents to the Jewish faith follow the teachings in the Torah, while Hindu religion has the Bhagavad Gita to serve as their guide for proper conduct. For the Navajo, originally an oral culture without writing, their sacred guide is embedded in the land, in some cases literally written in stone. Ever present in the day to day lives of the people, these sacred places—in combination with the stories associated with them—constantly remind the Navajo about proper conduct.

The sun-bleached bones of children who misbehaved lie atop Spider Rock in Canyon de Chelly. Red Mesa was stained with the blood of the Monster Déél-gééd, who was punished by Monster Slayer for murdering people with his breath and then eating them. These are not just simple stories told with laughter around a campfire. Rather, they are moral guideposts that teach how to avoid misfortune and gain protection in an unpredictable world. The land and the stories associated with them teach of right and wrong, good and evil, and continue to have meaning in today's industrial world. Because Big Snake kept pushing the drill bit out of the earth, an oil company had to halt exploratory drilling at Navajo Blanket Mountain. Thunder and lightning caused the crash of a military aircraft that flew too close to Thunderbird Mesa. Perhaps foremost among proper conduct for the Navajo is also considered proper conduct in other world cultures: One must not disregard the Holy People, or their wrath will destroy you. For the Navajo, this wrath is expressed by being driven from the land and sent into exile, as were the Anasazi—a harsh fate indeed.

Notes

1. See <www.lapahie.com/Sacred_Mts.html> for pictures and a discussion of the Navajo's major sacred mountains.

2. Details differ as to whether or not First Man and First Woman brought soil with them, or had to send animals back to retrieve the soil. As can be expected with any kind of oral narrative passed down through the generations, a great deal of variation exists as to the specific details of Navajo creation stories.

3. John Ford's first movie filmed in Monument Valley was *Stagecoach*, starring John Wayne, in 1939. If you watch this film, don't be fooled—the Indians you see are Navajo portraying Apache, and Geronimo is not known to have ever visited Monument Valley.

4. Many of the Navajo teachers at Diné College do not like the description of Coyote as a Trickster figure, because in their view this term does not adequately express his importance. Instead, to the Navajo Coyote represents the concept of disorder, as the opposite of order, balance and harmony. In the story recounted here, the state of greed is a state of disorder. To be avoided when possible, disorder is inevitable in the world, and can be corrected through ceremonies.

The National Historic Preservation Act 4

THE POST–WORLD WAR II ERA saw rapid population growth and industrial expansion in the United States. Not only did this postwar industrial boom affect the Navajo economy, it made impacts all over the United States and around the world. Urban buildings from the late 1800s and early 1900s were razed to make way for newer, bigger, more modern structures. Rural land, containing numerous archaeological sites, was turned into housing subdivisions and strip malls. This expansion, while good for the economic growth of our nation, also meant the unchecked destruction of unique and irreplaceable cultural resources important for understanding and appreciating our American heritage. In 1966, the federal government passed the National Historic Preservation Act in order to manage the loss of these cultural resources. This legislation created the National Register of Historic Places—a listing of properties and objects that hold significance to our collective society (see papers in Carmichael et al. 1994 for a discussion of legislation designed to manage or protect sacred sites in a variety of countries around the world).

Section 106 of the National Historic Preservation Act is one of the most important sections for archaeologists, historians, and Indian tribes. Section 106 specifies that when a "federal undertaking" occurs, the impact on all properties eligible for the National Register must be taken into consideration. A federal undertaking is considered to be any activity that

1. Occurs on federally controlled land [e.g., National Forests, National Parks, Bureau of Land Management, Bureau of Reclamation, military installations, Army Corps of Engineers transportation and flood control on river systems];
2. Constitutes any private development project that requires a federal permit or uses any federal funds [e.g., strip mining for coal, Interstate highway projects, block grants, or loans for housing construction].

Development projects on Indian reservations—other than development initiated internally by the tribe and using tribal funds exclusively—requires federal as well as tribal approval. As such, most development on reservations is considered a federal undertaking.

Not surprisingly, Indian lands have also experienced population and industrial growth, accompanied by the inevitable land destruction of the post–World War II era. Reservations are in need of roads, electric and sewer lines, housing, schools, and commercial shopping facilities, all of which alter the land. Indian reservations are also often actively involved in minerals extraction, which can provide significant income to the tribes in the form of royalties, as well as important employment opportunities for tribal members. Thus, it is important to recognize that Indian peoples are not living on park-like reservations that are removed and carefully protected from the modernization and development issues that impact the rest of American society.

However well-intentioned the National Historic Preservation Act was when initially created, in time it came to focus mostly on the scientific and professional interests of archaeologists and historians (King 1998). Mostly, properties listed on the National Register were the grand homes and public buildings of wealthy, prominent, Anglo-Americans, or archaeological sites with important research potential. Native American communities were not the only ones whose sacred or otherwise culturally relevant geography—traditional cultural properties[1]—went largely ignored (Parker 1993). Indeed, many properties associated with rural, African-American, and other ethnic communities remain unrecorded and unevaluated for listing in the National Register. In part, the under-representation of many Indian-related locations on the National Register is because many are natural landforms that have cultural and religious significance, but do not contain human constructions, such as buildings or other kinds of tangible, physical remains of the past. In 1992, important new amendments were made to the National Historic Preservation Act that seek to make the National Register more meaningful and useable for all members of American society. Indeed, Section 101(d)(6)(A) makes it unmistakably clear that properties of traditional religious and cultural importance to an Indian tribe or Native Hawaiian organization may be determined eligible for inclusion in the National Register.

The 1992 amendments did not make such properties eligible for the first time. The amendments sought to remedy the unfortunate and ethnocentric reality that federal and state agencies had been narrowly interpreting the original law, usually to the detriment of minority properties. The 1992 amendments made it clear that cultural resources needed to be interpreted in a much broader sense to include sacred and other cultural locations of all Americans. As we shall see, however, there are problems associated with interpreting cultural resources in this broad manner (Parker and King 1998).

In addition to clarifying existing legislation, the 1992 amendments also provided for important new changes. Perhaps one of the most important of these changes allowed for the creation of Tribal Historic Preservation Offices. Prior to 1992, state agencies created by the National Historic Preservation Act—State Historic Preservation Offices—were responsible for overseeing the impact on cultural resources during federal undertakings not only on state land but also on all Indian reservations within their state borders. Because of the direct federal government to tribal government relationship established by treaty, many tribes resented state oversight of their lands in regard to their cultural resources.

Since 1992, on a tribe by tribe basis, some or all of the functions of the State Historic Preservation Office can now be taken over by tribal governments. This provision gives the tribe more control over the cultural resource decision making process, rather than having a State Historic Preservation Office make such decisions for the tribe. Indeed, State Historic Preservation Officers, despite their usually well-meaning attempts to adhere to federal law, have often been seen by tribes as state interlopers who threaten tribal sovereignty (Holt 1990). Of the 556 federally recognized tribes,[2] more than thirty have created Tribal Historic Preservation Offices[3] to date.

In addition to reservation land, Indian nations often retain an actual and legal interest in land within the tribe's external reservation boundaries or their tribally ceded lands. In the course of European expansion across North America, Indian people were forced to give up—to cede—their lands, and move to reservations with precisely defined boundaries. Legally binding treaties were written that specified the land to be given up—the tribally ceded land. Often, hunting and fishing rights were legally retained by treaty even though the land itself was ceded. The external boundaries of a reservation define the original outer limits of the reservation before sections were carved out by such means as the 1887 General Allotment Act, also called the Dawes Act (Deloria and Lytle 1983). The Allotment Act gave each Indian head of household 160 acres and 80 acres to single individuals, in hopes that tribal cultural orientation would be weakened by individual land ownership. Any land not allotted to individual Indians was opened up for white settlement, and created such historical events as the Oklahoma Land Rush of 1889 that grabbed nearly 2 million acres of Indian land in less than nine hours. Even though white settlers purchased some the land during this time, such land still falls today within the legal external reservation boundaries and hence is subject to greater Indian control than land that was never part of a reservation.

The reality, however, is that Indian control over current reservation land is usually much, much greater than over tribally ceded land, land within a tribe's external boundaries, or over legally defined aboriginal use areas awarded to tribes through the Indian Land Claims Commission.[4] At least in the Southwest, Indian reservation land is often surrounded by federal or state land, where governmental agencies have control over development and cultural resource management, even though that land may overlap with tribally ceded land, a tribe's external boundaries, or aboriginal use areas. For the Navajo as well as for many other tribes, off-reservation concerns center mostly on religious sites and repatriation[5] issues. Off reservations, it is not unusual that

> . . . [F]ederal agencies either make no attempt to identify traditional cultural properties or make what tribes consider to be an inadequate effort. Hopi and Zuni, for example, insist that National Historic Preservation Act compliance activities within their traditional use areas require identification, assessment and evaluation of traditional cultural properties, and that only tribal members have the expertise to provide these services. Federal agencies often do not agree with this approach, sometimes maintaining that fieldwork is unnecessary, that any tribal participation must be supported by tribal funds, or that the tribe has no legitimate connection to the project area. Tribal disagreements with State Historic Preservation Officers usually revolve around the application of significance criteria and the evaluation of traditional cultural properties (Anyon, Ferguson and Welch 2000, 132).

Huerfano Mesa, the home of First Man and First Woman, and later of Changing Woman and the Twins, is the symbolic center of Navajoland. Huerfano Mesa, however, is not on the Navajo Reservation and today it sprouts a thicket of electronic communication towers (Jett 1995). Despite protest from the Navajo, they were powerless to stop the development due to its location off-reservation, under Bureau of Land Management jurisdiction. On a brighter note, in 1967 the Bureau of Land Management proposed to turn the eastern wing of Huerfano Mesa into a major recreation area. Again, the Navajo protested, and this time they were able to negotiate an agreement with the Bureau whereby the eastern wing of the mesa is now off-limits to anyone other than medicine men and their guests (Linford 2000, 219). Such successful negotiations were unusual in the 1960s, but they have become more common since the passage of the 1992 amendments.

Taken together, the 1992 amendments to the National Historic Preservation Act make it clear that native peoples are, by law, active participants in the federal land management process on relevant tracts of land, and in matters concerning the treatment of their human skeletal remains and other kinds of sacred and cultural artifacts currently held in museums. Further, it is now unmistakably clear that the National Register is not limited to the physical manifestation of past activities, that is, archaeological or historical sites, but also includes locations of spiritual or cultural significance to all segments of American society. To be eligible for listing in the National Register, traditional cultural properties do not need to contain physical remains such as artifacts or structures; in fact, it is quite possible that they do not contain such remains, as many such locations were considered too sacred to be used in the same manner as other places.

With the 1992 amendments to the National Historic Preservation Act, the Navajo were one of the first tribes to create a Tribal Historic Preservation Office. As such, the Navajo have led the way in establishing policies and procedures that often serve as blueprints for tribes who are in the process of creating their own Tribal Historic Preservation Offices. Clearly, tribes that have established their own preservation programs are in a much stronger position to apply their own interpretations of significance concerning archaeological, historic, or natural landforms that hold cultural or religious value to the tribe.

The National Register of Historic Places

The National Register is an actual listing of historic places.[6] To date, there are over 71,000 listings. The list is maintained by an individual within the U.S. Department of the Interior, National Park Service, in Washington, D.C. Each state has a National Register Review Board operating out of the State Historic Preservation Office. Although the Review Board operates from the State Historic Preservation Office, it is independent of that office, and free to make its own recommendations concerning eligible properties.

To be eligible for listing in the National Register a property should be at least fifty years old, and must possess other conditions such as "integrity" (i.e., not be overly disturbed by human or natural elements), and must meet one of the following four criteria:

Criterion A: The property must have an association with events that have made a significant contribution to the broader patterns of our history.

Criterion B: The property must have association with the lives of persons significant in our past.

Criterion C: The property must be distinctive of a type, period, or method of construction; be representative of the work of a master; or possess high artistic values.

Criterion D: The property must have yielded, or have the potential to yield, information important in prehistory and history.

Graceland, Elvis Presley's Memphis home, is on the National Register under Criterion B. Gettysburg, the site of a major Confederate defeat during the Civil War, is on the National Register under Criterion A. Fallingwater, a product of Frank Lloyd Wright's architectural genius, is on the National Register under Criterion C. Most smaller and less spectacular archaeological and historic sites are on the National Register due to their scientific research value, which falls under Criterion D. Properties may be eligible for inclusion on the National Register based on more than one criterion.

Again, the 1992 amendments clarify that even places associated with events that cannot be proven with scientific techniques—that Spider Woman taught the Navajo how to weave at Spider Rock—are eligible for inclusion in the National Register. Such places are most likely to be eligible for the Register under Criterion A. As long as the event is generally understood to be the traditional history of the group, and the belief is clearly associated with a specific location such as Spider Rock, then that location is eligible for listing in the National Register. Such locations continue to be important today because their preservation helps maintain the cultural identity of the community holding that belief. Spider Rock may also be eligible for the National Register under Criterion B, because Spider Woman— whether historically proven to have once been alive or not—is significant in Navajo culture, and is associated with that specific location. Although many traditional cultural properties in this country concern Native American traditional places, Irish American, African American, Italian American, Mexican American, Asian American, or even just plain old American traditional cultural places are also eligible for the National Register, assuming they meet the eligibility requirements.

The Section 106 Process

The Section 106 process of the National Historic Preservation Act is implemented through regulations contained in 36 CFR,[7] Part 800. Just because a property is listed or is eligible to be listed on the National Register does not mean that the property cannot be altered or destroyed. Through the Section 106 process, potential impacts of federal undertakings to eligible properties are considered, but the properties themselves are not necessarily preserved. The primary goal of the National Historic Preservation Act—through the Section 106 process—is to find a mutually agreeable balance between development needs and valuable cultural resources. Ideally, this goal—through compromise on both sides—produces a win-win outcome for all parties involved.

The management of properties listed or eligible to be listed on the National Register means that certain procedures must be followed before the property can be altered or destroyed. These procedures usually entail a combination of research and documentation techniques: excavation, mapping, photography, architectural drawings, the recording of oral histories associated with the property, and perhaps the taking of permanent samples, before the alteration or destruction can occur. These procedures are negotiated and agreed upon by the State Historic Preservation Officer and the relevant federal agency official before the property can be altered or destroyed. In the case of the Navajo Nation, the Tribal Historic Preservation Officer is the central figure in these negotiations, instead of the State Historic Preservation Officer, for any federal undertaking on Navajo Nation land. For federal undertakings off current Navajo Reservation land, the State Historic Preservation Officer retains the central role, even when the issue centers on impacts to Navajo traditional cultural properties on federal land that the Navajo occupied prior to European arrival.

When a federal undertaking could alter or destroy cultural resources, the Section 106 process, along with the Secretary of the Interior's standards,[8] requires that a series of steps be followed. The first step in this process is commonly a records review followed by an inventory of all cultural resources in the project area. These inventories, as well as subsequent steps, are usually carried out either by private consulting companies or university or museum contract personnel that have archaeologists, historians, and perhaps cultural anthropologists on staff. Even if the actual work is contracted out to a private consulting company, the federal agency overseeing the undertaking retains the authority and the responsibility for adequately complying with the National Historic Preservation Act.

As part of the first step, an archaeologist (typically) visits the area to be altered or destroyed with the goal of first finding and then recording the cultural resources that are threatened. The ground surface is walked to locate any visible structures such as historic homesteads. If ground visibility is poor, as is often the case in forest or pastureland in the eastern United States, shovel probes at specified intervals will be dug to locate any subsurface artifacts. This kind of fieldwork will occur across the entire land area slated for impact by the federal undertaking. A report of findings is then written. This report provides an inventory, detailing the number of sites found, their exact location, size, and as much information about site contents as can be determined from the survey.

At this stage, the archaeologist tries to assess the significance of the sites. Significant sites can be large and spectacular or they may be small and unremarkable. Significance sometimes hinges upon how much is already known about that type of site in the region. If a particular type of site is very common in the region, the archaeologist may determine it to be insignificant, whereas if the site type is relatively uncommon, the archaeologist may consider it to be significant, and thus potentially eligible for listing on the National Register. Sometimes, archaeologists may actually rank the sites (Reed 1987; Wilson 1990). At the bottom of the ranking are sites that could be destroyed and, we believe, our ability to understand and appreciate the past would not be hindered very much. Thus, these sites are considered ineligible for listing in the National Register. At the top of the ranking may be sites that the archaeologist believes are eligible for listing on the National Register. Somewhere in the middle of the ranking are "indeterminate" sites. These sites require more work before the archaeologist is willing to place the site into an eligibility category for the National Register. The inventory and assessment report is presented to the State/Tribal Historic Preservation Office. Staff members at the State/Tribal Historic Preservation Office read the report, perhaps visit some sites for themselves, and either completely concur with the federal agency's assessments of sites, or may suggest that the federal agency change some of the assessments.

Sites that have been deemed insignificant, and thus ineligible for the National Register, can then be destroyed by the federal undertaking. Indeterminate sites will then go on to the next step: evaluation. During the evaluation step the archaeologist will return to the site for a number of days, or perhaps a number of weeks for a large site. Test excavations will occur, more shovel probes will be dug, and for historic sites, architectural evaluations and archival research may also be done. At the end of the evaluation fieldwork, another report is written summarizing the additional information, and new assessments of site significance are made based on the expanded information. The State/Tribal Historic Preservation Office will review this report, and will either concur or not concur with the federal agency's findings.

If both the federal agency and the State/Tribal Historic Preservation Office agree that a site is eligible for listing in the National Register, a number of things could then happen. The simplest possibility is that the site could be avoided—the road passes over a different ridge; the pipeline runs along the other side of the valley (of course, the different ridge and the other side of the valley would also need to be surveyed for significant cultural resources). Assuming that the federal undertaking is in an early stage of the planning process, avoiding properties is the best possible scenario—the cultural resource is not destroyed and money is not spent that could be used elsewhere. A win-win outcome is easily achieved for both the cultural resource and the proposed development. However, in many instances, a cultural resource cannot easily be avoided.

Again, it is important to stress that even if a site or other cultural resource is listed or is eligible for listing on the National Register, it does not mean that the federal undertaking that would impact the cultural resource must be halted. Rather, National Register listing or eligibility for listing simply ensures that, by law, measures must be taken to consider the property and lessen its impact on the property. Precisely how the impact can be lessened—known as the mitigation of adverse effects—depends on the nature of the property, the nature of the proposed disturbance, and the individuals negotiating the mitigation measures.

The mitigation of adverse effects is the final step in the Section 106 process. This final step is sometimes referred to as the data recovery step prior to the actual impact of the federal undertaking—often some kind of major land alteration or destruction. Mitigation usually involves extensive and time-consuming excavations that are usually expensive. If the site is large and complex, many months of excavations may occur with many more months of laboratory analysis and report writing to follow. People must be paid, tests such as radiocarbon dating must be run, specialists must often be contracted for bone and botanical analyses, and laboratory and computer facilities must be maintained. Who pays for the mitigation? If the undertaking is on federal land, either taxpayers or the private company proposing the undertaking pay for mitigation costs. If the undertaking is not on federal land but requires a federal permit, the private company—the coal contractor, the logger, or the gravel quarry operator—pays for the mitigation.

As much information as possible is salvaged from the site during the mitigation, or data recovery step. After the mitigation has been completed, the bulldozers may be allowed to destroy what remains of the site within the project area, and the undertaking proceeds. Thus, through the Section 106 process, National Register-eligible cultural resources are not necessarily preserved, but rather, the negative impact resulting from their destruction or alteration is lessened through mitigation—the scientific removal of data. Through data recovery, the adverse impacts are considered acceptable to the scientific community, even though the resource itself may be destroyed in the process. Even though compromise and negotiation may be a long and difficult process, the goal of the National Historic Preservation Act is a win-win outcome for all affected parties, even though the federal agency retains the authority and the responsibility for actually deciding the final outcome. A win-win outcome, however, does not mean that all affected parties will be completely satisfied.

In the foregoing discussion, the cultural resource under consideration is assumed to be an archaeological site or another type of historic property such as a historic building. Indeed, these are exactly the kind of properties that have proliferated on the National Register because of their tangible, relatively easily assessed nature. These properties also have had a whole host of professional, full-time advocates as watchdogs over their interests. Traditional cultural properties, on the other hand, are harder to both document and evaluate in regard to significance and thus evaluate for listing on the National Register. Indian and other minority-oriented sites also do not usually have full-time advocates to look out for their interests. As such, traditional cultural properties remain underrepresented on the National Register. Since such properties remain either unlisted on the Register or not considered eligible for listing, they may be missed when the Section 106 process is carried out. Thus, traditional cultural properties are often not afforded the same degree of attention as is usually the case for archaeological sites and historic properties.

Documenting and Evaluating Traditional Cultural Properties

Sadly, the usual point in time in which an inventory of cultural resources—be it archaeological, historical, or traditional cultural properties—occurs is once planning for a land-altering project is well under way. At that late stage in the process, such resources are often regarded as nuisances by the project developer. The law and regulations encourage the project sponsors to initiate the Section 106 process early in the planning procedure, to provide ample time for real and substantive consultations with affected parties. With early planning, parties such as an Indian tribe can help in the initial project design to avoid culturally sensitive areas from the outset, rather than having to deal with them later in the project (Banks, Giesen, and Pearson 2000, see also Downer and Roberts in Parker 1993). The management of cultural resources should be proactive, rather than reactive. As project planning proceeds, design alternatives are eliminated, and each advance in planning reduces the amount of flexibility in consideration of alternatives, which increases the likelihood that interests cannot be accommodated later in the development process (Downer 2000, 55).

Some tribal governments have started to compile inventories of their traditional cultural properties well in advance of land-destroying development. Such prior action enables the tribe to do more than merely respond after the fact, when the properties are already threatened. For example, the State Historic Preservation Office in New Mexico is in the process of creating a Geographic Information Systems (GIS) database for nonreservation land that will contain information concerning kinds and locations of traditional land use, traditional cultural properties, and information concerning how and when each tribe wants to be contacted depending on the property and the nature of the proposed development. Such an endeavor is ambitious, but is exactly the kind of long-term planning tool necessary for the National Historic Preservation Act to achieve its goals.

The consideration of traditional cultural properties and their eligibility to the National Register becomes even more complicated when the dimension of time depth is added. Given the very fluid nature of prehistoric as well as historic population movements, current reservation land, tribally ceded land, or land with the external boundaries of a tribe, these properties may have had a whole host of previous Indian owners. As such, the traditional cultural properties of the previous occupants need to be acknowledged and honored through the Section 106 process every bit as much as do the traditional cultural properties of the current occupants.

The Navajo Reservation contains traditional cultural properties important in Navajo culture, and also traditional cultural properties important to other tribes. Indeed, when the Navajo Nation recently initiated a major new effort at intertribal consultation, they contacted thirty-four neighboring tribes with an invitation to be involved in consultation regarding cultural resources on the current Navajo Reservation (Downer 2000). Although some tribes are concerned with only certain areas of the Navajo Reservation, the Hopi are most actively involved in the ongoing consultation process for cultural resources—traditional cultural properties in particular—on Navajo Nation lands. Given the complexities of the Navajo–Hopi Land Dispute, such consultation can at times lead to disagreements about the best way to handle a given property. Although the Navajo engage in active consultation with other tribes concerning their traditional cultural properties, ultimately it is the responsibility of the Navajo Nation, as the current landowner, to make decisions concerning properties in their jurisdiction. Similarly, federal agencies such as the National Forest Service—while by law are required to make a good-faith effort to consult with tribes such as the Navajo—are also responsible for making the final decision concerning properties under their jurisdiction. Not everyone will be happy all the time.

Confidentiality

Typically, documentation for traditional cultural properties includes items such as tape recordings or written notes of oral interviews with elders, medicine men, or other traditional culture bearers. Photographs, drawings, field notes, and primary written records that establish the properties as having been important in the historical past can also be part of the documentation. However, traditional people may be unwilling to divulge sacred information to outsiders, or commit it to paper, or allow the resource to be photographed or recorded. There are a number of important reasons for this secrecy (see also Gulliford 2000).

One reason for the secrecy is the power of the information itself. "In an oral tradition, the stories about the land contain . . . almost a set of instructions on the proper care and use of the land. You don't willingly pass such instructions to anyone whom you don't want to use the land" (Kelley and Francis 1994, 3). Thus, silence is often the first line of defense—obviously, one would not willingly tell a burglar how to open a safe full of valuables. Additionally, it is only appropriate to share such information in the context of a long-term apprenticeship relationship, and in the case of some of the most powerful stories or songs or prayers, only when the teacher is about to die. Sometimes, supernatural retribution—death, illness, or misfortune—may result for the individual who makes such a transgression. Important issues may also not be discussed simply because "the indiscriminate spread of knowledge lessens its power" (Kelley and Francis 1994, 3).

This kind of secrecy, however well-reasoned, can pose major documentation problems for federal agencies that must provide rationale for their actions. How can a property be managed and protected if there is no one there who knows it or is willing to say why it is important? If the federal agency is willing to be flexible, however, creative reporting of sensitive information can be arranged. Examples of creative reporting may include reports that document sensitive information only in detachable appendices. Navajo Nation traditional cultural property reports are often handled in this manner, allowing certain key, decision-making individuals— and those individuals only—to read confidential information. With the appendix detached, others can read the report without compromising either individuals who provide information or the information itself. This kind of reporting format may give traditional individuals the security they need to be willing to reveal sensitive information. Thus, sensitive information can be kept restricted by the tribe, a particular religious society, or a particular clan, thus balancing the need for confidentiality with the need to protect important resources in the face of often necessary and desired economic development. Another alternative to detachable appendices is to have religious representatives of the tribe read a draft of the report, striking or rewording any information that the tribe does not want made public.

Sometimes it may not even be necessary for a tribe to divulge specific information about traditional cultural properties. For example, the U.S. Air Force, in planning for the deployment of the MX missile system in Wyoming, was made aware that the Lakota tribe considered the area to contain traditional cultural properties (Parker and King 1998). The Lakota, however, were unwilling to provide details about where the properties were, and why they were sacred. The Air Force met with the Lakota and showed them a variety of possible building sites. The Lakota, in turn, were able to choose the areas they would like to have avoided, but without giving specific reasons. Because Air Force plans were still in the early stages, they were able to avoid those locations without even knowing why they were sensitive. Both the Lakota and the Air Force were satisfied with the outcome. This approach worked in this instance because both parties came to the table with a willingness to negotiate, and because of early consultation. Clearly, each case is different, and varied approaches are needed depending on the specifics of each situation.

Variability

As is common with any oral transmission of information, variation emerges in repeated telling through generations. Whose information is correct? The idea that one can simply walk into an Indian community, ask for *the* traditional culture bearer, and be straightforwardly told *the* story surrounding a particular place, is far from reality.

For example, we know that Spider Woman taught Navajo women how to keep their people warm by weaving blankets. However, details around the teaching vary. Some individuals say that women should put their whole soul into the weaving (Oughton 1994), while other individuals say that they should not put their soul into it, because it causes the weaver to become too prideful (Duncan 1996). In fact, it is even possible for one individual to tell different versions at different times, according to the context of the cultural need. For example, if someone is being boastful about their weaving, they may hear one version of the story, but if someone is being lazy with their weaving, they may hear the other version, from the very same person. Culture can be flexible in the way it allows individuals to believe two apparently contradictory things at once.

Variability in detail is to be expected. In fact, the reported location of even something as seemingly basic as the Navajo's sacred mountain of the east, Sisnaajinii, is variable (Van Valkenburgh 1974, 189–90). Sisnaajinii lies far away from the modern Navajo Reservation. In general, the further one lives from the area asked about, the more imprecise the answer; for example, people from the western area of the reservation will not be as familiar with the eastern reservation. However, just because its modern location is not always agreed upon does not make its existence any less important to Navajo culture. Too much variability in the main story, however, may suggest that a particular traditional cultural property may not be as central to the belief system of a people as other stories that have less variation. But, a lot of variation could also mean that a place is critical to many segments of a society that have slightly different uses of a place and different historical relationships with that place. Thus, the degree and nature of the variability must be carefully assessed during the evaluation process.

Field Methods

It is important to realize that some variability in informants' responses may in fact be due to inconsistent field methods on the part of the interviewer. In a group of studies aimed at constructing an inventory of traditional cultural properties at various locations on the Navajo Reservation, Kelley and Francis (1994, 60) identify the broad range of methods that can be employed.

The studies differ mainly in what groups of people they focused on, how they chose people to focus on from within the group, how structured were the interviews, and whether they verified the locations of places with maps, field visits with or without interviewees, and so forth.

To date, there are no accepted guidelines for conducting traditional cultural property interviews. Rather, to a certain extent at least, everyone reinvents the wheel. Agencies may set some guidelines that their cultural resource staff should follow, while individual tribes may set other guidelines for their employees. Private consulting anthropologists may create their own methodology. Sometimes, tribes may arrange for traditional culture bearers to work with the interviewers for several days at a stretch. The traditional culture bearers are familiar with the kind of work being done, are prepared to provide a wide range of information, and are paid for their time. In other studies, however, the interviewers rely on finding local residents (who may or may not be traditional culture bearers) at home during the day. These interviewers spend a highly variable amount of time (from five minutes to perhaps several hours) asking them about important places in their area.

It is not uncommon for cultural anthropologists to use questionnaires, in large part to make each interview consistent and thus comparable. Questionnaires are not common in traditional cultural property interviews, however. "To use questionnaires gives the interviewer the superior, controlling role in the discourse and is therefore disrespectful of the elders and the medicine people, as well as inconsistent with the way requesting the gift of valuable knowledge subordinates the interviewer" (Kelley and Francis 1994, 63).

The amount of time researchers have and the size of the land they need to cover, also have a bearing on the methods they use. Does one try to interview all the residents in a study area, even if they are not traditional culture bearers? Does one try to find culture bearers that may not actually live in the area but nevertheless have esoteric knowledge about it? These questions are important because the particular methods employed in any kind of research may themselves account for differences in the results, thus making the results difficult to interpret. Differences in methodology also mean that comparison among traditional cultural properties for National Register evaluation purposes becomes more difficult.

It is also very clear that the lack of consistency may derive in part from the lack of funding and understaffing within tribal cultural resource programs themselves. Recognition of the problems, assessment of how to improve field methods, the creation of new procedures, and organizing the actual implementation of the new procedures requires both sufficient staff and monetary resources. Understaffing is a problem in all agencies, but is nowhere more pronounced as in tribal cultural resource programs (Downer 2000). It is impossible to be everywhere and do everything at once.

Invisibility

Documentation usually involves current photographs and maps of the property and drawings of how it may have looked in the past. Drawings may also be made of how the property may look in the belief system of the culture that considers it sacred. For example, Navajo medicine men may be asked to draw Spider Woman's invisible web as it stretches across Canyon de Chelly. Is her web attached to Spider Rock, and if so, how and where on the rock? Combining invisibility with variation for a moment, although individual medicine men may envision the size, location, orientation, and weave of Spider Woman's web differently, does not mean that the property is any less significant.

Interconnectedness and Unclear Boundaries

Where a traditional cultural property begins and ends is also not always easy to determine. How does one place a clear boundary around a mountain slope from which ceremonial sage is collected? Indeed, to traditional Native American philosophy, all land is sacred, although some locations—such as those associated with particularly important supernatural beings or events—are considered more sacred (Jett 1995). If it can be done at all, determining which locations are more sacred requires much consultation within the tribe itself.

Kelley and Francis (1994, 42) advocate a landscape, rather than a piecemeal, approach to the protection of traditional cultural properties. A landscape approach focuses on the fact that sacred places are not isolated entities that exist apart from one another. Rather, they are interconnected, all tapping into the same protective and healing power of the Holy People. The landscape approach to traditional cultural properties usually involves considering a much larger area of land than just the immediate project area. Federal agencies prefer the piecemeal approach to traditional cultural properties. This approach seeks to define discrete, tidy boundaries that are clear and unambiguous. Such a definition of boundaries does not fit well with Indian views of these traditional places, although it would, for example, enable a logging operation to avoid a precise area. Fitting Indian beliefs into the needs of federal agencies is like trying to fit the proverbial square peg into a round hole—the fit will always be imperfect, from both the Indian and the agency perspective.

Kelley and Francis suggest that consideration must be given to how land-disrupting development can fit into landscapes that have linked, interconnected sacred places, with the least disruption possible. Rather than trying to deny the interconnected nature of cultural landscapes, agencies need to work with the concept, rather than against it. For example, Spider Woman only learns of disobedient children from Talking Rock, who is located across the canyon from Spider Rock. If some new development were to block Talking Rock's communication with Spider Woman, she may no longer be able to provide the tough love necessary to keep Navajo children in line. If medicine men indicate that the communication is mostly verbal, then auditory disruptions such as logging or mining may be particularly undesirable kinds development that could alter the sound qualities of the area. Other kinds of less noisy development may be somewhat more palatable.

Another, even more land-extensive example of linked traditional cultural properties is Navajo Mountain. Navajo Mountain is on the Navajo Reservation, in the state of Utah. Navajo Mountain is said to be the head of a woman, Black Mesa her body, Tuba Butte and Agathla Peak are her breasts, Comb Ridge and a raised area near Marsh Pass are her arms, and Balakai Mesa are her feet (Linford 2000, 300). It is even said by some that the Carrizo, Lukachukai, and Chuska mountains form a reclining supernatural male figure. Lying together, male and female land forms lie side by side, making love. Others say the male and female lay head to toe, in the traditional sleeping position of a comfortably married Navajo couple (Preston 1995, 128).

Setting

What about a logging operation immediately adjacent to the mountain slope where ceremonial sage is collected? Road access, noise, and visual impacts as experienced from the sage-collecting area are all relevant issues. Since ritually used plants are usually collected with songs, prayers, and offerings, development projects that intrude on sage collecting—even from outside the actual area—negatively impact the continuance of traditional activity. In addition to the National Historic Preservation Act, the American Indian Religious Freedom Act of 1978 guarantees access to religious sites and mandates consideration of those sites in federal land use decisions. As we will see, however, this latter act has much more bark than bite.

Significance Period

It is often important to determine how long a property has been considered sacred or culturally significant. The response may be something like "since time immemorial." This response should be included in the documentation, along with any information that archaeology can provide: Is there a religious or resource-oriented site on the property that can be dated? Do historic records note the special nature of this location? Documented current use of the site for similar purposes is also helpful. For example, do people still visit Spider Rock to make offerings and say prayers?

Conclusion

As should be clear by this point, the typical archaeologist or historian is not well trained to record and assess traditional cultural properties. Indeed, it is likely that more cultural anthropologists will begin working in the field of cultural resource management, a field that has long been dominated by archaeologists. There will also be an increasing role for Indian consultants in this field. Indeed, the 1992 amendments to the National Historic Preservation Act encourage the broadening of cultural resource management not only in the conceptualization of what constitutes a cultural resource eligible for the National Register, but also in personnel. Both of these changes will require considerable, ongoing adaptation and maturation of the historic preservation profession as it plays its pivotal role in finding win-win outcomes for all parties.

And finally, even though there are inherent difficulties in documenting and evaluating traditional cultural properties for listing on the National Register, it does not mean that they can be ignored by archaeologists, tribes, or by the land managers of federal agencies. Indeed, a subsequent chapter discusses how a federal agency—the U.S. Forest Service—sought to downplay the importance of traditional cultural properties in regard to a ski resort in northern Arizona. Unfortunately for the Forest Service, the ski resort rests on the slopes of the Navajo's sacred mountain of the west, *Dook'o'oosłííd*, adorned by First Man with abalone shell and fastened firmly, high up in the sky, with sunbeams.

Notes

1. Traditional cultural properties are also sometimes called traditional cultural places. The use of "places" serves to more closely link the concept with a particular location on the land. In cultural resource management literature, however, the term "properties" appears to be more common, and thus is used here.

2. For current listing of federally recognized tribes, see Department of the Interior, Office of American Indian Trust, "American Indians and Alaska Natives," <http:/128.174.5.51/denix/public/Native/outreach/American/indian.html> (accessed February 24, 2002).

3. The number of Tribal Historic Preservation Offices is expected to grow in the years ahead. For a current listing and contact information, please see Advisory Council on Historic Preservation, "Tribal Historic Preservation Officers," <www.achp.gov/thpo.html> (accessed February 24, 2002).

4. The Indian Land Claims Commission was an official attempt to right past wrongs—the seizure of Indian land by various kinds of government action—treaties, warfare, outright theft, or other congressional acts. The Navajo filed their claim in 1951, claiming compensation for 17 million acres taken in the Treaty of 1868 without due payment (Acrey 1998, 282). Although the claim was approved in 1970, the fair land value in 1868 has yet to be determined and just compensation rendered. Even when land claims are approved it is rare that land is actually returned to the tribes. Instead, monetary compensation is usually provided and hunting, fishing, and other traditional use and consultation rights to traditional cultural properties may be established over the original land. Land claims litigation is still ongoing for many tribes. For information on specific land claims cases, see chapter 19 of Indian Land Claims Settlements, Legal Information

Institute: U.S. Code Collection, <www4.law.cornell.edu/uscode/25/ch19.html> (accessed February 24, 2002).

5. Repatriation of human remains, funerary and sacred objects, and items of tribal cultural patrimony held in federally funded museums and collected on federal and Indian land, is mandated by the Native American Graves Protection and Repatriation Act (NAGPRA) passed in 1990. See "National NAGPRA Database," National NAGPRA: National Park Service, National Center for Cultural Resources, <www.cast.uark.edu/other/nps/nagpra> (accessed February 24, 2002).

6. To find out what properties in your community are listed in the National Register of Historic Places, see the National Park Service, <www.cr.nps.gov/nr/> (accessed February 24, 2002).

7. CFR stands for Code of Federal Regulations.

8. For more detail about these standards and guidelines, see the Secretary of the Interior's "Standards and Guidelines for Federal Agency Historic Preservation Programs Pusuant to the National Historic Preservation Assistance Program," <www2.cr.nps.gov/pad/sec110.htm> (accessed February 24, 2002).

Natural Resources, Economic
Development, and Navajoland

5

THE NAVAJO TRIBAL GOVERNMENT, like all governments, is interested in providing a high standard of living for their people. Historically, the Navajo defined wealth and a high standard of living as one based primarily on a large sheep herd. Population growth, economic changes, overgrazing, and increasing aridity, however, have made a traditional herding and farming lifestyle difficult to sustain. Indeed, there is no longer enough grazing land for everyone, and only one in six Navajo families holds a permit to graze sheep (Tolan 1989). Thus, even if they so desired, for most contemporary Navajo actually living in the traditional way on a day-to-day basis is now impossible. As such, we see the five-fingered Earth Surface People caught in the shift from a traditional horticultural-pastoral economy, to the market-driven economy of an industrial society. In this light, they are similar to global cultures elsewhere who are also making this often difficult transition (see Bodley 1994).

In an industrial society, a high standard of living entails such things as quality health and educational facilities, electricity, water, sewer, roads, and perhaps most important of all, access to employment opportunities. Indeed, throughout the 1970s and 1980s, four-term Tribal Chairman Peter MacDonald's most urgent priority was economic development (Iverson 1983; Shapiro 1988). He promised to bring up to 2,000 new jobs a year to the reservation. His successors have continued this nontraditional, pro-capitalist, industrial-oriented philosophy. Although some important successes have been made in this direction, as we will see below, internally generated tribal revenue is still almost exclusively produced through natural resource extraction. The BIA has consistently encouraged this kind of energy development, and Navajo tribal leaders have continued in this direction.

The Navajo standard of living, compared to that of non-Indian America, remains low. Per capita income in the United States is 4.5 times higher than on the

91

Navajo Reservation, meaning that over half of the reservation population lives below the poverty line (Choudhary 1999, 12). Around 40 percent of Navajos on the reservation are estimated to live without electricity and even more live without running water.[1] Overall formal educational attainment remains low, with only a 44 percent high school graduation rate (compared with an 86 percent high school graduation rate for white Arizonans in 1990 [Choudhary 1999, 56]). Navajo health problems still consist mainly of diseases that stem from a poor diet, primarily type II diabetes and heart disease (Yazzie 1999). The transition away from traditional garden and livestock-based foods—mutton stew, fry bread, and blue corn meal mush—to a store-bought, high sugar, high fat diet has not been beneficial for the Navajo. Smoking rates are high. Accidents leading to death, primarily drunk driving related accidents, are much higher than the overall U.S. average. Indeed, alcohol-related deaths among Indians aged fifteen to 24 are seventeen times higher than the national average.[2] Other poverty-associated problems such as alcoholism, substance abuse, suicide, teenage pregnancy, split families, and minor crime all contribute to a continuing low standard of living on the reservation. Clearly, economic development that creates jobs, eases poverty, and addresses social issues is not an unreasonable goal of the Navajo Tribal Council.

Given the stark realities of the Navajo economy, the tribe finds itself wrestling within a difficult catch–22 situation: Natural resource extraction brings money into tribal coffers to support a variety of programs, including bilingual, bicultural programs. Natural resource extraction entails land-altering development. Land-altering development means that traditional cultural properties will be threatened and perhaps destroyed. Finally, threatened traditional cultural properties rock the very foundation upon which Navajo culture rests, a culture whose identity is defined in part by their relationship to the land.

Unemployment

One persistent problem is unemployment. In 1997, the unemployment rate[3] for Navajos living on the reservation was at 58 percent, over ten times higher than the rest of the nation (Choudhary 1999, 10). A number of causes contribute to chronic unemployment on the Navajo Reservation. One reason is the minimal number of private enterprises—Navajo-owned or otherwise—on the mostly rural reservation. This is a problem small communities of any ethnic background face in all parts of the country. On Indian reservations, this problem is exacerbated due to the difficulty Indian people face in obtaining bank loans to open and run a new business. Since reservation land is held in trust by the federal government, neither the tribe nor individual tribal members actually own the land. Since the land is not considered private land, it cannot be used as collateral when applying for a regular bank loan (Aberle 1983b; Russell 1999).

A related issue is the extreme quantity of red tape involved in opening a private enterprise on the reservation. Again, since Indian reservations are considered federal trust land, the BIA—a federal agency—must approve all development. Since there is a sovereign tribal government, development decisions must also be approved at the tribal level. Thus, two levels of bureaucratic red tape must be maneuvered for a business to even start. Upon their expiration, renewals of such business site leases are not necessarily straightforward and are far from guaranteed (Choudhary 1999). This reality discourages any but the largest private companies from setting up their businesses on the reservation: McDonald's, Burger King, Taco Bell, and Texaco. It is large companies such as these that are able to take the risk of having their business leases revoked. The risk taken by these big companies is outweighed by the benefits of a lack of competition—few restaurant options means more income for the restaurants that do exist. In addition to federal and state taxes, the tribal government also taxes businesses. Given such constraints, small-scale entrepreneurs often view investment prospects on Indian reservations as unattractive.

Even Navajo entrepreneurs are unable to ease or to speed the process. As a result, small businesses—Navajo and non-Navajo alike—sprout up and prosper in the border towns surrounding the reservation. For example, David John, a Navajo hairdresser, tried for six years to start a hair salon business on the reservation. Finally, he gave up and within weeks was operating a salon off-reservation in Farmington, New Mexico (Shapiro 1988). Thus, energetic and talented Navajo who have a mind toward business find it difficult to acquire the requisite permits and capital that private individuals elsewhere in the nation can much more easily obtain. While a high percentage of Navajo work in off-reservation businesses, they must either commute long distances, live off-reservation, or maintain two residences, none of which are attractive prospects. Living and working off-reservation also means that income earned by Navajos flows into Anglo-owned companies, rather than recirculating within the Navajo Nation, creating other jobs in the process. In 1997, an estimated 61 percent of personal income earned by Navajos was spent off-reservation (Choudhary 1999). Thus, there are considerable down-the-line, long-term consequences of unemployment on the reservation, not the least of which may be accelerated culture loss.

Pending legislation may create reservation enterprise zones[4] that would make development easier on reservations. A brainchild of the Commission for Accelerating Navajo Development Opportunities (CAN-DO), this legislation would create tax incentives for private business operations, and a special Indian Development Bank to guarantee loans. Similar to Export Processing Zones in many Third World countries, they would be set up to facilitate the operation of private businesses on reservations. Such economic systems have not been without their critics,[5] and it is unclear whether such zones would help reservations in the long run, although the industries themselves usually benefit greatly.

In 1989, the State of Arizona designated Navajo and Apache Counties, portions of which are on the Navajo Reservation, as Arizona Enterprise Zones (Choudhary 1999,28). Incentives include tax credits for state and property taxes. Arizona Enterprise Zones are of primary benefit to non-Navajos businesses, since Navajos do not pay state income tax or property taxes on reservation property. In 1993, President Clinton signed the Indian Investment and Employment Tax Incentives-Omnibus Budget Reconciliation Act, which provides various kinds of tax incentives to businesses that relocate or expand onto Indian reservations. More pending legislation, specifically Senate Bill 2052, would greatly cut federal red tape by streamlining paperwork (*American Indian Report*, November 2000,16–17). This bill, if passed, would enable tribes to complete one set of paperwork, rather than numerous sets, each slightly different, depending on which federal agency is involved. Thus, numerous strategies are either in place or pending to change the negative economic environment for private business on the reservation. Only time can judge the success of these programs.

Some tribes (actually only a small minority of the federally recognized tribes) have turned to gambling casinos as a solution to their employment and poverty problems. Out of the twenty-one tribes in Arizona, seventeen have gaming operations. The Navajo, however, have twice voted down gambling on their reservation, once in 1994 and again in 1997, due to strong opposition from the traditional community (see Henderson and Russell 1997 for more discussion of the Navajo gaming issue). Recently, however, the Tribal Council has given approval for the tribe to enter into negotiations with the states of Arizona and New Mexico to acquire a compact to conduct gaming. The gaming ordinance was pushed in large part by Tohajiilee Chapter representatives.[6] The Chapter is about twenty miles west of Albuquerque, where it will be the first casino encountered along the interstate, thus casino construction expenses could be easily recouped from gambling profits.

The Navajo Nation's annual budget consists of the external budget and the general fund. Revenue flowing into the external budget comes mostly from federal (and some state) government funds, to meet obligations such as education, healthcare, and social services expenses. These obligations stem both from the Navajo's Treaty of 1868, but also from numerous subsequent executive orders pertaining to all federally recognized Indian tribes. The Navajo general fund consists of internally generated revenue that the tribal government can use as it sees fit. An example of a general fund program the tribe has recently created is the Navajo Traditional Apprenticeship Program. In operation since 1998, the program provides a small stipend ($300 a month) to tribal members to complete their training in certain ceremonies that are on the verge of extinction. A total of 125 men and women are either in the program or have completed it.[7] Another pressing need on the Navajo Reservation is road improvement. During heavy rainfall the rural dirt roads turn into quagmires of mud, and are virtually impassable. The Tribal Council has earmarked money specifically for road improvement, but with a very rural, dispersed population, muddy roads will remain a feature of reservation life for some time. Certainly, there is no limit to the number of programs that are deserving of financial support.

The monetary health of the general fund fluctuates wildly. For fiscal year 2000, the general fund composed one third of the overall budget. For fiscal year 2001, however, the almost $110 million general fund made up only one eighth of the overall Navajo Nation budget.[8] This dramatic change reflects both the shrinking of internal sources of revenue, as well as an increase in external funds. The shrinking of the general fund—which supports many valuable tribal programs that are not supported by external sources—is occurring despite a growing Navajo population that requires and demands greater services. As has long been true, much of the general fund revenue comes from oil, gas, and coal mining operations. In 1999, an astounding 65 percent of the general fund was based on these three kinds of natural resource extraction (Choudhary 1999, 3). And, as with all finite resources, logic dictates that this situation cannot last forever, highlighting the fact that the current economic strategy is short term at best (Aberle 1983b).

Again, it is a sad irony that these land-altering, natural resource extraction activities directly threaten traditional cultural properties, which in many ways embody the essence of Navajo culture. Nevertheless, the reality is that these resource extraction activities generate much needed revenue to support tribal programs, many of whose goals include the preservation of traditional Navajo culture. This irony also pits tribal members against one another. Caught between the proverbial rock and a hard place, internal tribal divisions are often expressed through groups that consider the protection of traditional cultural properties as primary, and groups that see the generation of revenue as the more pressing goal. Clearly, there is no easy answer here. The Section 106 process, however, with the integration of traditional cultural property work, seeks to bridge such divisions and negotiate a way to do both—to have one's fry bread and eat it too.

Industrial Development on the Navajo Reservation

In 1868, when the Navajo were allowed to return to their land from Bosque Redondo, it was land that Anglo-Americans considered relatively expendable. The land was arid, full of steep cliffs, and contained neither gold nor silver in any quantity. In recent years, new kinds of land-based wealth, largely unanticipated in 1868, have become astoundingly valuable. This wealth is in the form of petroleum, coal, uranium, and timber, among other natural resources. Indeed, the Navajo Nation is fortunate among Indian peoples for the natural resource endowment they possess.

Unlike much private land where mineral rights are often severed from surface rights, Indian tribes never lost the mineral rights to their land. Like reservation land itself, however, reservation mineral rights are also under United States trusteeship, overseen by the Minerals Management Service. In its position in the Department of the Interior,[9] the Minerals Management Service is one of eight federal bureaus whose concerns include water, wildlife, and the land itself. Through these bureaus the country's natural resources are managed. To manage resources means to exploit them responsibly. What the owner of an oil company defines as responsible exploitation, however, may be wildly different than how even the average citizen defines it. Together, the Minerals Management Service and the BIA must organize and approve the exploitation of reservation natural resources. It has been suggested that the BIA occupies the lowest rung in the Department of the Interior (Chamberlain 1998). If the BIA were to aggressively protect Indian mineral resources, they would be in direct conflict with other, stronger bureaus in the Department that are more oriented toward natural resource extraction (Reno 1981).

Thus, it is not always clear whose interests the BIA is safeguarding — Indian interests, or big business and government interests (through increasing tax money). In 1975, for example, the BIA negotiated annual payments for a natural gas pipeline at only $40,000. Navajo attorneys renegotiated and instead received $500,000 in annual payments (Nugent 1975). Clearly, Navajo energy resources were worth far more than the BIA was willing to demand. It took courage and steadfastness from the tribe to renegotiate the value of their natural resources, rather than allowing the BIA to "guard the henhouse" for them.

Regardless of who guards the Navajo henhouse, royalties from energy leases provide the vast majority of revenue for the general fund, thus enabling the support of a wide variety of worthwhile and much needed programs on the reservation. The current reality, however, is that the tribal government's general fund is supported by the depletion of tribal natural resources. A further reality is that the monetary gain derived from natural resource extraction often takes priority over traditional cultural properties—the physical manifestation of Navajo culture itself.

Petroleum

Petroleum—oil and natural gas—is undoubtedly one of the most valuable natural resources on the Navajo Reservation (Baars 1995). Oil is refined into gasoline, which enables America's suburban sprawl, and also into home heating oil, which keeps us warm in winter. As early as 1922, the Midwest Refining Company had identified several locations, had applied for and received Navajo Tribal Council approval, and had successfully drilled their first well in the Shiprock District. Many more oil wells were to follow. Since that time, the Santa Fe Corporation, Continental Oil Company (Conoco), Gypsy Oil Company, Producers and Refiners Corporation, Pan American (AMOCO), Continental Oil Company, Western Natural Gas Company, Southern Union Gas Company, Shell, Texaco, Kerr-McGee Corporation, and others have all profited from petroleum reserves under Navajo land.

Beginning in the early 1950s, exploration and drilling reached a frenzy following the discovery of the Aneth Oil Field, north of the San Juan River in Utah. With the discovery of Aneth—one of the larger oil fields in North America—the Navajo Nation decided it had the right to a greater percentage of the wealth produced from its land. Mineral rights and royalties, the latter previously standardized at 16 percent, were put up to sealed bid auctions to the highest bidders (Baars 1995; see also Chamberlain's 1998 dissertation on Navajo Oil). The wealth earned by the Navajo Nation was tremendous. Other tribes, particularly in Texas and Oklahoma, also benefited from renegotiating leases during the oil boom. While these latter tribes took the path of distributing the wealth directly to its individual members, the Navajo spent the initial earnings as a tribe, financing schools, hospitals, chapter houses, roads, tribal businesses, and tribal parks.

When individual payments finally began in the mid-1960s, the traditional mode of transportation, the horse-drawn Studebaker wagon, disappeared as if by magic, and pickup trucks swarmed on the reservation. Truck dealers in nearby towns became financial tycoons. Oil had made its mark in Navajo Country (Baars 1995,164).

Since the 1966 National Historic Preservation Act, oil extraction even by private industries is considered a federal undertaking and must be permitted by the federal government. For example, the location of drilling pads and the linear path of the pipeline to transport pumped oil or natural gas needs to be surveyed for cultural resources that would be impacted. Road access to drill pads is also included in the area to be impacted. Since the mid-1990s, traditional cultural properties have also been addressed in these federal undertakings. In these instances, the company, as part of the cost of doing business, absorbs the compliance costs associated with these federal regulations. As long and linear constructions, pipelines traverse great distances and cross a wide variety of terrain. Fortunately, due to the linear nature of these lines, they can be re-routed relatively easily to avoid important features of the landscape.

Coal

Vast quantities of Navajo coal are burned to generate electricity. The electricity is then transported via high-tension transmission wires to cities such as Los Angeles, Las Vegas, Phoenix, Tucson, and Albuquerque. Since coal leases were renegotiated in the 1980s, coal has overtaken oil as the most valuable natural resource on Navajo lands. In 1992 coal production exceeded 25 million tons, and still-abundant coal reserves remain on existing leases.

Coal is economically most valuable when it is of high quality and is easily accessible near the earth's surface. The top of Black Mesa and the edges of the San Juan Basin are two locations where topographic conditions permit easy surface mining due to relatively shallow soil overburdens. Although the stripped land is reclaimed—reconstructed and revegetated—such tampering with the land is not acceptable to many Navajos.

> It is not the land their ancestors grazed and farmed; it is not the land that generations of Diné nurtured and loved; it is not the land that contains the bones and ghosts of their ancestors or those gone before. This restored land is different, unnatural, and morally unpalatable. Who would ever call such rebuilt and reshaped land home? What would the ghosts of their ancestors think? What would the Holy People think?[10]

Coal is also most economical when burned near its source, with the resulting energy transported through wires. Water is also a necessary element of electrical

Figure 5.1.   Author's photograph of the Four Corners coal burning power plant, near Page, Arizona.

generation. This has meant the construction of very large coal-burning generators near Page, Arizona, to burn the Black Mesa coal, and near Shiprock, New Mexico, to burn the San Juan Basin coal. These two generating facilities in particular have greatly damaged the air quality of the region. Scrubbers are to be integrated into the Page generating plant that will reduce sulfur dioxide emissions; to date this integration has not been completed.

In addition to surface mining, since the mid-1960s Peabody Coal has been using a slurry line to transport coal out of the region.[11] The slurry line transports pulverized coal using water from underground aquifers. The slurry itself consists of 50 percent coal and 50 percent water. The eighteen-inch steel pipeline originates at Peabody's Black Mesa processing plant, and traverses 275 miles to the Mojave power plant at Bullhead City on the Colorado River (Mails and Evehema 1995). There, the water is centrifuged out and the coal is burned to produce electricity. It is estimated that 7,500 acre-feet of water is used annually in this process. The Navajo and Hopi tribes are compensated $1.67 per acre-foot; for comparison purposes, the Central Arizona Project for Water Use receives $55.00 per acre-foot for the use of their water. In a region with eight to fifteen inches of annual rainfall, it is not surprising that the continuous use of such a huge quantity of water has severely reduced the amount available for irrigation farming, livestock, and general domestic use.[12]

Since the federal government regulates, companies must obtain a permit from the Office of Surface Mining. The act of permitting by a federal agency makes coal mining a federal undertaking, and the Section 106 process is triggered. In the late 1960s, Peabody Western Coal Company leased the surface mineral rights to the northern end of Black Mesa from the Navajo Nation. From 1967 to 1983, fieldwork for the Black Mesa Archaeological Project surveyed 256 square kilometers of land, identifying approximately 2600 archaeological sites (Gumerman 1970; Gumerman, Westfall, and Weed 1971; Spurr 1993). Over 220 sites were considered potentially eligible for the National Register, and were either partially or completely excavated over this 16-year period. Due to its extent and duration, the Black Mesa Archaeological Project represents one of the largest archaeological undertakings in the United States. Although Navajo period sites were recorded in the Black Mesa project, there was no formal effort to identify traditional cultural properties in the area to be stripped, since traditional cultural property interviews only became standard practice after the 1992 amendments to the National Historic Preservation Act.

In 1990, Peabody received another federal Office of Surface Mining permit to expand mining in the same area surveyed during the original Black Mesa Archaeological Project. However, since the original survey work, the Native American Graves Protection and Repatriation Act (NAGPRA) had been passed, which now required Peabody to first list and then mitigate archaeological sites likely to contain human burials. This list was compiled using a predictive modeling program based on the earlier Black Mesa work. The model predicted that burials are most likely to occur on late period sites that have midden deposits and kiva architecture. Thirty-two sites fit this description, and were excavated in the early 1990s to fulfill NAGPRA regulations. A total of thirty-two individuals and their associated grave goods were excavated. Limited analysis was performed on the remains before they were reinterred. All of the cultural resource compliance work described here was paid for by Peabody.

As we have seen, coal mining impacts water levels, may destroy archaeological and traditional cultural properties, intrudes upon human burials, lessens air quality, and disturbs the original ground surface. Traditional Navajo in particular are unhappy about these impacts. On the important flip side of the coin, of course, is the fact that coal extraction produces money for the tribe. Tribal leaders, however, often feel pressure to increase tribal income. In 1998, Peabody Coal signed the papers providing an additional $35 million in royalties to the Navajo over a ten-year period. A $2 million signing bonus was also part of the deal. Although these sums are impressive, it is important to keep in mind that they represent a fraction of the coal's value in the national marketplace. Coal royalties and signing bonus monies go directly into the Navajo Nation general fund, to support worthy projects such as increasing bilingual, bicultural education and medicine man apprenticeships. In addition, jobs are created:

Figure 5.2.   Author's photograph of sign for Peabody Western Coal Company, Black Mesa, Arizona.

Peabody Western Coal Company has 706 employees, 642 of whom are Navajo, providing an important source of local employment in an economy characterized by unemployment.

Uranium

The nuclear generation of electricity is produced through bombarding a nucleus of uranium until it splits, producing large amounts of heat in the process. It is said that one gram of fissionable "yellow cake" uranium could produce as much heat as three tons of high-quality coal (Baars 1995, 176). Despite the promise of high and inexpensive energy production, the safe extraction, fission, and disposal of the spent uranium remains a major problem. The element is abundant on the Navajo Reservation, particularly along the Grants Uranium Belt of northwestern New Mexico (Reno 1981).

Although uranium was known to exist in the region, it was the desire to build nuclear weapons during World War II that spurred its initial mining. In the immediate aftermath of the devastating stock reduction program, uranium extraction appeared as heaven-sent. An added attraction was that Navajo men did not have to travel off-reservation to find wage labor, and of course by this point Navajo families had become increasingly dependent on external sources of income. From 1948, when the United States Atomic Energy Commission started purchasing uranium, to the mid-1970s, more than 55 million tons of uranium ore were mined from the San Juan Basin alone. Monument Valley has also been an important uranium-producing region, as has the Cameron area in the southwest corner of the reservation. As with oil and coal, the Navajo Nation was able to renegotiate uranium leases beginning in the 1960s, bringing millions of new dollars into the general fund.

As with most raw material extraction—and perhaps uranium in particular—the market is unpredictable. In 1971, the Atomic Energy Commission stopped buying Navajo uranium due to a saturated market. The 1980s and 1990s saw a dramatic drop in demand for uranium, on the heels of a moratorium on new nuclear power plant construction after the 1979 nuclear accident at Three Mile Island in Pennsylvania. Finally, the unpredictable nature of raw material extraction is now particularly unmistakable in the current era of globalization—the majority of uranium currently used in American nuclear power plants comes from cheaper, foreign sources. Despite a 1992 Navajo Nation moratorium on uranium mining on the reservation, it is possible that such mining may take place again.[13]

A legacy of uranium mining—undeniably apparent since the mid-1970s—has been an extremely high rate of birth defects and cancer linked to radon gas and radiation exposure. In 1990, Congress finally acknowledged that miners should be compensated for their losses. In order to get compensation, however, it was necessary for

Figure 5.3.   Laura Gilpin, *A Worker in a Uranium Mine on Top of the Lukachukai Mountains, Arizona*, gelatin silver print, Aug. 24, 1953, © 1979, Amon Carter Museum, Fort Worth, Texas, bequest of the artist.

miners to provide documentation of their illnesses through evidence such as dates and locations of employment in the mines, and detailed medical records. Although such documentation does not at first seem unreasonable, in the Navajo context it is difficult to obtain (Brugge, Benally, and Harrison 1997; Eichstaedt 1994). Employment, then and now, tends to be temporary and sporadic and may in fact have been "under the table." Even when companies did provide documentation of formal employment, Navajo workers may not have kept such documentation, particularly since the 1940s. Finally, many miners may not have sought western medical care for their ailments, and since medicine men do not generally provide written summaries of their services, more often than not the required documentation cannot be provided.

In 2000, Congress amended the 1990 Radiation Exposure Compensation Act, easing documentation requirements, expanding the kinds of cancers covered, and allowing residents in more areas to make claims.[14] Overall, despite the increased compensation and revenue for the general fund, uranium mining turned out to be a disastrous solution for raising the standard of living and quality of life for members of the Navajo Nation.

Timber

Although many people believe the Southwest to be a dry and treeless land, large tracts of high-elevation forest exist on the Navajo Reservation, particularly in the Chuska Mountains that straddle the reservation near the New Mexico–Arizona border (Linford 2000, 1). Desert scrubland is found over the majority of the reservation, containing sage, greasewood, and other grasses, with minimal timber possibilities. At around 6,000 to 8,000 feet, juniper, piñon pine, scrub oak, aspen, and various species of fir and spruce appear. These trees are valuable for pulp and paper and other wood products such as particleboard. At around 7,500 to 10,000 feet, large stands of ponderosa pine and other evergreens are found. Comprising around 8percent of reservation land, these timber stands are highly valuable, particularly for cabin logs, telephone poles, and saw lumber.

Beginning with the first portable sawmill brought to the reservation in 1880, millions of board feet have been cut to provide housing materials for homes across the nation. In 1953 the Navajo Forest Products Industries was created as a tribal government enterprise to oversee timber production on the reservation. By the mid-1970s, timber assets were valued at over $26 million. In order to capitalize on the higher profits and increased employment of the secondary processing industries associated with logging, the tribal government built a new sawmill, particleboard plant, and a small furniture factory. Indeed, the new town of Navajo at the base of the Chuskas was created because of the logging industry. In addition to a public library, dental offices, a trading post, and a restaurant, the town boasted the first swimming pool on the reservation. Many new jobs were created both in the timber industry itself and in the service sector that sprung up around the timber industry.

Overall, timber production was highly profitable for the tribe. The tribal government's objective was the "development of the Navajo forest to its fullest productivity in perpetuity" (Reno 1981, 95). The perpetuity of forest production, however, was under serious challenge from two directions. One of these challenges was from livestock grazing. Livestock grazing—a time-honored pursuit that in many ways defines traditional Navajo culture—destroys young tree growth and thus reduces future prospects for continued forest-based profits. Here again the Navajo find themselves at an interesting philosophical juncture: Do they reduce or eliminate livestock herding to save the profitable forest industry, or do they allow herding to continue, and reduce the profitability of the forest, thereby diminishing revenue prospects for the general fund? The question, of course, goes much deeper than simply livestock versus trees. Rather, the answer to the question goes straight to the heart of the future course of Navajo culture—will it actively retain its traditional roots or will it set policies that allow or even encourage tradition to fall by the wayside? This is a classic example of the culture clash at the root of the transition from a traditional to an industrial economy. Thus far, few societies have found a solution to this problem that is palatable for all segments of the society, and the Navajo are no exception.

Beginning in the late 1980s and early 1990s, the tribal government was sorely criticized because it over-emphasized timber production at the expense of traditional uses such as grazing, ceremonial use, and traditional plant collecting, and by ignoring traditional cultural properties in the areas to be logged. In one instance, a local community succeeded in stopping a logging operation on a pair of sacred buttes on Changing Woman's route to the west. Indeed, it was this incident that forced the tribal government to conduct traditional cultural property interviews as well as archaeological surveys prior to land-altering development. This practice had originally been requested by the Medicine Men's Association (Kelley and Francis 1994, 158), but was only instituted by the tribal government under public pressure.

The other serious challenge to the Navajo timber industry is closely related to the traditional use issue. Throughout the same period, Diné CARE (Citizens Against Ruining our Environment, formerly called the Diné BiWilderness Society), a Navajo environmental group formed in response to the logging. Diné CARE brought heavy public pressure to bear on the negative environmental impact of logging as it was being practiced by the tribal government. Although aspects of this environmental conflict can be understood similarly to local issues anywhere—a kind of NIMBY (Not In My Back Yard) issue—in the Navajo context, the players have an added dimension that serves to bring an additional layer of complexity to the mix. This additional layer, of course, is one centered on culture and lifestyle—whether one values Navajo tradition or not. No Navajo politician would ever dare to even whisper that he did not value Navajo tradition.

Given the apparent incompatibility of logging with traditional uses, critical environmental questions, and monetary mismanagement of the tribal enterprise itself, logging stopped in the forest in 1994 (Pynes 1999). Today, the sawmill at the town of Navajo stands idle. Around 250 employees lost their jobs, the sacred buttes are unharmed, and countless trees remain standing.

Tourism: Antelope Point Marina

Obviously, resource extraction usually means the destruction or alteration of land that contains both archaeological sites and traditional cultural properties that may hold great cultural value. Increasing tourism is often suggested as a means of generating income that is minimally disruptive and that can be sustained over the long run. Although tourism may be minimally destructive of the land, it may be quite destructive for traditional culture and lifeways, particularly those linked to specific spots on the land. The Navajo tribe is interested in increasing tourism, and has made important strides in this direction, including allowing more restaurants, hotels, and gas stations on the reservation. Although these tourist-related facilities are important, they do not capture the lion's share of tourist dollars.

Plans for an important new tourist venture are currently underway, and are generating much controversy within the tribe. Lake Powell, created by Glen Canyon Dam, is a major recreation area, primarily for boating. The construction of Glen Canyon Dam in the early 1960s itself created much controversy for the Navajo, as many sacred sites were flooded as the water levels rose behind the dam. Despite tribal protests and lawsuits, Rainbow Bridge, the largest known natural sandstone arch in the world and a traditional cultural property of major significance, was also partially flooded.[15] Before Lake Powell was created, the Bridge was protected by its remote location; now, a two-hour boat ride brings anyone within an easy walk of the arch. In 1995, the National Park Service—the federal agency responsible for administering Rainbow Bridge National Monument—announced a voluntary ban on walking up to or underneath the Bridge. This has kept many tourists from coming too close to the Bridge, but certainly not all.

Lake Powell's southern edge borders the Navajo Reservation. In an effort to capitalize on the thousands of tourists that visit the lake for recreation, the tribal government is interested in constructing a tribally owned marina—Antelope Point Marina—on reservation land. The $60 million project calls for a hotel, 150-space RV site and a 50-space tent campground, boat services, a restaurant, a grocery store, a Laundromat, and an amphitheater. Although the rest of the Navajo Reservation is dry by continued vote of the Navajo people, alcohol sales are planned at the marina. Recently, however, the Medicine Men's Association has made a formal protest to the government concerning the marina plans.[16] Rather than opposing the project outright, the medicine men wish to have a new Environmental Impact Statement (last conducted in 1986) and a full and open discussion of alternatives.

Once again, we see the clash between traditional needs—the culturally proscribed long-term care of traditional cultural properties and land and lifestyle overall—and nontraditional needs—increased tribal revenue in the shrinking general fund. No one has clear answers to such difficult issues, and it is certain that no resolution is within easy reach. The best solution currently available is to follow such instructions as the National Historic Preservation Act has lain out.

Tribal Development and Tribal Divisions

With the possible exception of the timber industry, the majority of economic development on the reservation centers on the extraction of nonrenewable natural resources. Despite the fact that such extraction has indeed brought some wealth to the Navajo, the majority of that mineral-derived wealth has not actually remained on the reservation. Rather, the majority of the wealth leaves the reservation through the multinational corporations that operate there. While primary industries are owned almost exclusively by non-Navajos, secondary (processing) and tertiary (service) industries are sorely lacking on the reservation (Russell 1999). As discussed earlier, those that do operate on the reservation also are mostly owned by non-Navajos. Although the tribal government has been able to negotiate favorable new leases and royalties on mineral rights, it is the participation in the actual ownership of industries that is most lucrative.

To own and operate an oil exploration, extraction, and refinery industry, for example, would involve great capital outlay and geological expertise that does not currently exist within the Navajo tribe. Secondary and tertiary industries also require both initial capital and management skills. As a result, Navajo that are employed in these industries generally work for Anglo-owned companies on the reservation, or in off-reservation border towns such as Gallup, Flagstaff, and Farmington.

The Navajo also have the concept of "economies of scale" working against them. One of the reasons multinational corporations have been able to succeed is due to the large scales at which they operate. Because they produce (or extract) in large volume, their production is more efficient. Anyone who has ever worked at McDonald's knows that it makes more sense to put lettuce, tomatoes, and mayonnaise on five buns at once, rather than putting the same ingredients on one bun at a time—the higher the output, the lesser the production cost per unit. For the Navajo to purchase costly and technologically sophisticated machinery and train tribal members to operate and service the machinery in the relatively small area of the Navajo reservation would be difficult, but not impossible. In the short run, such industries would undoubtedly operate in the red, needing to be supported by the tribal government. Yet in the long run these same industries could be profitable and provide opportunities to gain much needed skills and experience in management. However, the experience with Navajo Forest Products Industries suggests that success in such endeavors will be far in the future.

In many ways, the Navajo economy has much in common with the economies of the Third World. In both instances, development is geared toward natural resource extraction by multinational corporations, whereby the extraction occurs locally, but the transformation of the resource—and certainly its consumption—occurs elsewhere. That "elsewhere" of course, is in the rich, industrial nations that are home to multinational corporations. Like Third World economies, the Navajo economy is a cyclical, boom/bust economy dependent on a very small handful of nonrenewable resources whose value can fluctuate wildly with market demands. In such economies future income cannot be predicted, making long-term planning next to impossible. The wildly fluctuating Navajo general fund is a perfect example of this reality. As with many Third World nations, the single largest employer is government—25 percent of jobs on the Navajo Reservation are government (federal, state, or tribal) compared with 14 percent in the U.S. overall (Choudhary 1999, 11).

Although the Navajo Nation government is well aware of the vulnerable nature of their economy, it is a difficult pattern to reverse. The government has adopted plans designed to wean the economy away from resource extraction and into areas more oriented toward renewable natural resources such as timber and livestock, and also into manufacturing, service, and tourism. The goal is to use current revenue from land-altering natural resource extraction to create more sustainable, long-term economic growth for the Navajo people. It has yet to be determined how well this goal will be met, but if recent revenue sources for the general fund are any evidence, even medium-term prospects for outgrowing the resource extraction-based economy are doubtful.

The Navajo Nation is a good example of a dual economy in the transition from one kind of society to another. On one side, large, highly technological, multinational corporations involved in primary resource extraction typical of industrial societies dominate the economy. These kinds of activities produce large surpluses, at least for the owners of the companies. Many Navajo are involved with this side of the economy, but are usually employed in the lower paying, manual labor positions. On the other side of the dual economy the orientation is mostly toward simple subsistence on a day-to-day basis—the pastoral and horticultural lifeways of traditional Navajo culture. Those engaged in this side of the economy tend the garden plots and the small sheep, goat, and cattle herds, weave the labor-intensive Navajo rugs, and make the silver and turquoise jewelry for sale at the trading posts. These kinds of activities require low levels of technology, and do not produce large surpluses.

Participation in the different sides of the economy tends to be both a generational and geographical issue, and serves to define a major cleavage within the tribe. As was already clear even before the Long Walk and the Treaty of 1868, these divisions have been longstanding within the Navajo Nation, and center on how best to interact with the non-Indian world. It is obvious that these divisions continue today. Boiled down to their perhaps oversimplified essence, these divisions center not only on how Navajo people should live their lives, but also on the future direction of their collective Navajo culture.

Such tribal divisions have long historical roots. One group of Navajo was interested in having minimal contact with non-Navajo people, with the exception of the trader at the trading post. These Navajo wished to maintain their independence by living a traditional lifestyle centered on sheep herding and corn gardening. The rituals of the centuries were to be followed, and the sacred landscapes protected. Today, this traditionalist group tends to be less wealthy, live in more rural locations, may have a poorer grasp of English, and may be less educated overall according to western standards. Even though many traditional Navajo today are unable to practice an exclusive sheep herding and horticultural economy, their philosophical orientations nevertheless clearly remain rooted in traditionalist perspectives. Thus, although the presence of elderly individuals is an important component of the traditionalist Navajo segment, the cleavage itself is not one that will end once time has passed and the older generation is gone.

The other segment of Navajo society can be understood as a nontraditional segment. Since historical times this group was much more interested in interacting with the Anglo world economically, politically, and culturally. Members of this nontraditional group tend to live in the reservation towns, perhaps in the government tract housing communities. They may be employed in the border towns off-reservation, in resource extraction industries, or in government offices, all of which afford more contact with non-Navajo people. Overall they are better educated according to western standards, may not speak much Navajo, and may be widely traveled off-reservation. Many younger Navajo in this segment are no longer taught the culturally valuable traditional skills associated with a pastoral and horticultural economy. These nontraditional people tend to be more willing to exploit the natural resources of the reservation. Although traditional Navajo have a strong political base in the Tribal Council structure, actual tribal government employees tend to be nontraditionalist due to their lengthy off-reservation stays and their lack of interaction with local communities. These two segments of Navajo society—traditional subsistence and nontraditional industrial—represent two polar extremes and thus clearly simplify the more numerous and complex cleavages that constantly shift their positions within Navajo society. Some individuals may actually fit very well into one or the other extreme. More common, however, is that a continuum exists between these two extremes, with each Navajo occupying a distinct place on that continuum. An individual's location along this continuum changes over time, with age and experience.

This cleavage within the tribe has a strong bearing on the differing values placed on traditional cultural properties by tribal members. Not surprisingly, traditional individuals tend to place a higher value on traditional cultural properties than nontraditional Navajo. Although in many ways the tribe as a whole has benefited from the aggressive energy development of the last fifty years, some Navajos have benefited more than others have. While traditional people have indeed won important victories, such as the closure of the timber industry, overall, the nontraditional Navajos have been the clear winners.

Notes

1. "Navajos join forces with Sandia Lab," *Arizona Daily Star*, December 15, 2000.

2. "Plan to sell alcohol at casino stirs a caution," *Arizona Daily Star*, November 26, 2000.

3. This figure does not take into account the informal economy that is quite active on the reservation. Probably the best Navajo example of an activity in the informal economy is making and selling turquoise jewelry off makeshift tables and car hoods. Income from such activities is notoriously hard to measure.

4. For a history and review of the legislation that has yet to pass through Congress, see "A Tribal Governance Leap into a New Millennium," National Tribal Development Association, <www.ntda.rockyboy.org> (accessed February 25, 2002). Also see Darmon Darlin, "Rebellions on the Reservations," *Forbes*, May 19, 1997, <http://perc.org/newsindian.htm> for a discussion of the impact that de facto socialism—mostly tribal or federal government jobs—has had on reservations.

5. For a brief critical review of enterprise zones, see "What They're Saying about EZs," <www.urich.edu/~ezproj/april99/what.htm>, (accessed February 25, 2002).

6. "Council OKs Gambling Law," *Navajo Times*, October 18, 2001; "Gaming Is Official," *Navajo Times*, November 1, 2001.

7. "Officials Seek Traditional Medicineman Apprentices," *Navajo Times*, August 10, 2000.

8. "Navajo Budget Bigger," *Navajo Nation Messenger*, September 6, 2000; "Council Rushes to Adopt Budget," *Gallup Independent*, September 8, 2000.

9. For a review of the bureaus, see Indian Trust Management Information, U.S. Department of the Interior, <www.doi.gov> (accessed February 25, 2002). Please note that

due to a hacking incident in December 2001, access to Department of the Interior web sites has been restricted, pending updates in security features. Please check back for access to Bureau of Indian Affairs.

10. Baars 1995, 171.

11. For pictures and an account of the coal slurry, mostly from a Hopi perspective, see John Daugherty, "Dark Days on Black Mesa," <www.wildnesswithin.com/mesa.html> (accessed February 25, 2002).

12. "New Report by NRDC Shows Material Damage to N-Aquifer," *The Hopi Tutuveni*, October 31, 2000.

13. "Local Groups Hail Removal of Uranium Mining Research Funding," *Navajo Times*, November 21, 2001; "Families Coexist with Past, Future Threat of Uranium," *Navajo Times*, November 1, 2001.

14. "Radioactive Reservation," *Arizona Daily Star*, July 30, 2000; "Meetings Detail Uranium Law," *Gallup Independent*, August 14, 2000.

15. For photographs and discussion of Rainbow Bridge and its history, see Rainbow Bridge National Monument, National Park Service, <www.nps.gov/rabr> (accessed February 25, 2002).

16. "Out of Balance," *Navajo Times*, December 27, 2000.

Cultural Resource Management and the Navajo Nation

THE NAVAJO NATION was an early leader in the trend toward tribally operated cultural resource management programs. Beginning in the 1950s, even before the National Historic Preservation Act was written, the Navajo began hiring archaeologists to conduct excavations and surveys on their reservation lands and beyond. The intent of much of this early archaeological work was to provide legal proof of former occupancy as required by the Indian Land Claims Commission. In the 1960s, these archaeologists were transferred to the Navajo Nation Museum in Window Rock, and after passage of the National Historic Preservation Act in 1966, they began conducting Section 106 work, inventorying and evaluating cultural resources on the reservation prior to the land-altering development of federal undertakings (Klesert and Downer 1990; McManamon 1999).

In 1977, The Navajo Nation Cultural Resource Management Program came into formal existence to coordinate the Section 106 work on the reservation. With the passage of the Navajo Nation Cultural Resources Protection Act in 1986 and a growing amount of Section 106 work, this program was divided into two separate departments—the Navajo Nation Archaeology Department and the Navajo Nation Historic Preservation Department. Together, these departments conduct and coordinate the vast majority of Section 106 work that occurs on the reservation. These two departments are housed within the Division of Natural Resources, as part of the tribal government's executive branch.

Until the early 1990s the BIA had controlled and in some cases performed all of the cultural resource management work done by these two departments. Beginning in the early 1990s, the Navajo Nation was, after many struggles, finally successful in receiving a 638 contract (from Public Law 93-638, the Indian Self-Determination Act) from the BIA Navajo Area Office (Klesert 1990). The 638 contract allows the tribe to conduct the vast majority of what had formerly been BIA archaeological functions. The ability to make such contracts was a key part of Indian self-determination legislation passed beginning in the 1970s and continuing through the 1980s, as part of a larger, national trend toward tribal self-governance (Wilkins 1999, 61–63). Such contracting enables the orderly transition from federal domination of programs and services to greater control by sovereign Indian tribes. Funding responsibilities for contracted programs remain with the federal government.

Many tribal educational facilities, including Diné College, are run under a 638 contract, and the Navajo Nation is currently in the process of contracting Indian Health Services. Since 2000, the federal welfare program has been in Navajo hands under a 638 contract.[1] Thus, even federal services not directly provided by the BIA are contractible. Such programs are, at least in theory, internally managed according to native values, as long as they meet BIA standards. The BIA monitors all such contracted programs and, according to some Navajo, often does so with a very heavy hand.

Another watershed occurred for cultural resource management on the Navajo Reservation in 1996. As a result of the 1992 amendments to the National Historic Preservation Act, the Historic Preservation Department assumed all functions of all three State Historic Preservation Offices on reservation land. Since the Navajo Reservation encompasses parts of three states—Arizona, New Mexico, and Utah—the decision making process related to cultural resources was often complicated and unwieldy. Since 1996, the Navajo Nation Historic Preservation Department houses the Tribal Historic Preservation Office.

The main office for the Historic Preservation Department[2] is in Window Rock, with branch offices in Shiprock, New Mexico, and Flagstaff, Arizona. This department is organized into nine distinct programs that together coordinate the work of managing the variety of cultural resources that exists both within and beyond the reservation. The Traditional Culture Program oversees the protection of sacred sites, the repatriation of ceremonial and important cultural material under NAGPRA, as well as the reburial of repatriated skeletal material. A group of medicine men serve as a formal advisory council to the program, as well as to the department overall. A number of Navajo cultural specialists are permanent employees in the department and assist with various programs. These individuals are traditional Navajo tribal members that enable the Historic Preservation Department to develop and follow culturally appropriate policies.

The Navajo Nation Museum also falls under the Historic Preservation Department. The museum provides exhibits and educational programs on both natural and cultural history to the Navajo people. The Chaco Sites Protection Program consults with the National Park Service in the interpretation and management of Chaco Canyon, one of the most important and most frequently visited Anasazi archaeological areas in the entire Southwest. The Roads Planning Program manages cultural resources endangered through road construction. The Glen Canyon Environmental Studies Program works with the federal government concerning the protection and preservation of sacred and historic places threatened by the operation of the Glen Canyon Dam. The Forestry/Natural Resources Program coordinates Section 106 work prior to timber and other natural resource related undertakings. The Chambers–Sanders Trust Lands (the "New Lands" section of the reservation) Program works with Navajos relocated through the Office of Navajo and Hopi Indian Relocation, to identify cultural places within their new lands. The Facilities Management Program provides assessments and recommendations for the reservation's historic buildings, primarily trading posts, missions, and BIA boarding schools.

Finally, the Cultural Resources Compliance Section reviews Section 106 reports for compliance with the National Historic Preservation Act and the Navajo Nation Cultural Resources Protection Act. All cultural resource management work performed on the reservation, whether by off-reservation private consultants or by the tribal government's own consulting branch (the Navajo Nation Archaeology Department, see below) must be reviewed by this Section. The reviewer may require that any number of changes be made to a report. Such changes may range from altering the scale of a map to changing the assessment of eligibility to the National Register for a particular site. Recommendations for managing specific cultural resources as impacted by an undertaking are accepted, rejected, or modified. Will a road or a pipeline, as per the consultant's recommendation, reroute 100 meters to the west to avoid an archaeological site? Will logging not be allowed within three miles of a butte considered sacred by the local community? After reviewing and accepting the reports, the Historic Preservation Department then provides approval for the undertaking to proceed—the road can be built, the pipeline can be laid, or the logging may commence. It is through this compliance-related activity that the Historic Preservation Department plays a similar role to State Historic Preservation Offices elsewhere in the United States. Thus, the Historic Preservation Department houses the Navajo Nation's Tribal Historic Preservation Office, and the director of the department is the Tribal Historic Preservation Officer responsible for the management of cultural resources—including traditional cultural properties—on the reservation.

The Navajo Nation Archaeology Department[3] also has its main office in Window Rock, with branch offices in Flagstaff, Arizona, and Farmington, New Mexico. The Archaeology Department performs the majority of the actual archaeological and ethnographic fieldwork and report writing for cultural resource management that occurs on the reservation. While the Historic Preservation

Department is provided with federal funds through their 638 contract with the BIA, the Archaeology Department largely relies on individual contracts for its operation. Contracts come from a variety of sources: federal, state, or tribal governments; private companies (such as Peabody Coal); and private Navajo individuals who wish to build homes prior to the issuance of a homesite lease. Typical contracts obtained by the Archaeology Department for tribal or federal government undertakings include surveys prior to the construction of electric power lines or the laying of water lines to individual homes. Surveys prior to road construction or improvement are also performed through the Archaeology Department. Should an important cultural resource—either historic, prehistoric, or a traditional cultural property—be identified through survey, the Archaeology Department can perform the necessary excavations or other mitigation measures in order to lessen the adverse impacts of the undertaking. The Archaeology Department also works with tribal law enforcement officials to document and protect endangered sites from looters and vandalism.

Since their inception, Anglos at the top management levels have, for the most part, administered both the Archaeology Department and the Historic Preservation Department. Although Navajo professional staff have grown considerably in recent years and in many cases outnumber Anglos, the moment has not yet arrived that a Navajo individual, holding an advanced degree, has taken over as a department head. Currently, both Northern Arizona University in Flagstaff, Arizona, and Ft. Lewis College in Durango, Colorado, have cooperative programs with the Archaeology Department for student training programs. These programs provide hands-on training for Navajo (or other Native American) students working toward college degrees in anthropology (either in archaeology or ethnography). Rather than simply training competent field technicians, such programs seek to train supervisors capable of managing complex archaeological and ethnographic projects. In fact, in 2000, the Archaeology Department received an honors distinction through Harvard University's Tribal Governance Award.[4] The goal of the Archaeology Department's training program is to eventually replace all Anglo staff in both departments with qualified Navajo individuals. To facilitate this goal, the Navajo Preference in Employment legislation makes it clear that Navajo individuals are preferred over other ethnic groups in all areas of tribal government. The Navajo Nation—through the general fund—provides partial support for the Archaeology Department's student training program. However, due to the shrinking general fund, over the last five years there has been a 50 percent overall decrease in tribal funding for the student training program (Warburton 2000). Again we are confronted with the irony of the current reality: land-disturbing resource extraction provides revenue to the general fund, which in turn is the almost exclusive source of funding for many successful, worthwhile programs that support Navajo culture in general, including the enhanced management of traditional cultural properties.

The very positive and well-intentioned goal of integrating more Navajos into both the Historic Preservation and Archaeology Departments is not without its difficulties. One of the difficulties is cultural. Navajos in general—and traditional Navajos in particular—wish to have minimal contact with the physical remains of the dead, specifically human burials (Warburton 2000, 97–98). There is even an official Navajo Nation policy that clearly instructs that such material should be left alone. This aversion stems from Navajo beliefs concerning the soul (Ward 1980). Navajo do not fear death, but they do fear the dead. At death, part of the soul moves on to the afterlife, while part of it—the ghost part—remains near the place where the individual died. Ghosts can cause problems for living people, particularly when the living intentionally disturb the dead. For some traditional Navajos, even the arrowheads and pottery and homes of the dead should not be touched or visited, since the people who made them or lived in them are now dead. Anglo archaeologists—whose culture has no such prohibitions—are contaminated through their cumulative exposure to the remains of the dead. Such contamination can be dangerous for Navajo people, especially for pregnant women. As a result, many traditional Navajo students are not interested in pursuing archaeology as a career, and if they do, their family may request that cleansing ceremonies be performed for them on a regular basis.

Added to this cultural issue is the quite diminished standing of anthropology and archaeology among Native Americans overall.

At the most general level, anthropologists on the Navajo Reservation and elsewhere have usually been extractive in their studies. We have extracted data, information, personal histories, artifacts, and samples of every kind from Navajo people for our professional advancement, and have given back virtually nothing to the communities other than fractured and distorted visions of Navajo history and society. There are of course some wonderful exceptions to this pattern, including people who have worked in medical anthropology and land claims cases, but as a whole, anthropologists are considered a subspecies of humans in Navajo eyes (Warburton 2000, 97).

Thus, even while the Navajo Nation Archaeology Department's student training program has been successful, in some realms it is also controversial (see Two Bears 1999 for a Navajo anthropology student's perspective on these issues). Clearly, the goal of having Navajo individuals involved in cultural resource management is well-intentioned, but for many Navajo people it is not always an easy choice to make. Two significant hurdles need to be overcome for such individuals—cultural prohibitions against being near or handling objects associated with the dead, and the historically extractive nature of the discipline itself.

Differing Perspectives on Cultural Resource Management: Avoid or Mitigate?

Not surprisingly, the western industrial philosophies concerning cultural resources are different from the philosophies of nonindustrial (or currently industrializing), nonwestern, native people. Indeed, this philosophical difference no doubt extends to many other resources than just cultural resources.

In general, today's western industrial philosophy centers on information retrieval—data recovery—through scientific means: if the data can be obtained, then, if necessary for technological progress, the actual source of that data may be dispensed with. For Anglo-Americans, mitigation through scientific study lessens the negative impact to an acceptable level, and a win-win outcome is achieved. Nonindustrial, native philosophy tends to see cultural resources in a more holistic view. This view places the cultural resource itself—not just information about it—into a much more closely woven cultural fabric. This fabric defines and weaves together human social and religious responsibilities to the land with the supernatural beings that inhabit that land. Thus, human and supernatural responsibilities are reciprocal—humans perform the proper rituals and take proper care of the land, and the supernatural world will care for those human actors. In such a perspective, data recovery is irrelevant.

Tribes consistently advocate resource protection through avoidance of impact. In contrast, federal and state agencies see heritage resources as primarily tangible things and places that compete with other values and resources for management priorities. It is consequently common for nontribal agencies to advocate the treatment of a resource by mitigating impacts with a scientific data recovery program. Mitigation by scientific study is thus seen as a viable alternative to protection and avoidance (Anyon, Ferguson, and Welch 2000, 132–33).

Most American Indian tribes would strongly disagree with the notion that mitigation is a viable alternative to avoidance, especially when traditional cultural properties are the issue. In fact, rather than helping the situation, mitigation through scientific data collection is often seen as exacerbating the problem. Many tribes view such impacts as particularly negative when the mitigation itself either disturbs the dead or exposes esoteric knowledge or objects that are best kept private from the non-Indian community (Anyon, Ferguson, and Welch 2000; see also Begay 1997; Martin 1997). Thus, tribes do not commonly view data recovery through excavation prior to the undertaking as a win-win outcome, and as a result, the primary goal of the National Historic Preservation Act is not achieved.

From the western industrial perspective, unless a property holds outstanding cultural value, it can be sacrificed for the benefits the development offers. From the nonindustrial, Navajo, or other native perspective, unless the development itself holds direct and explicit value or benefit for the impacted community, the cultural resource should be preserved and the development dispensed with. Although the distinction may be subtle, it is of critical importance: For Native Americans, the onus is on demonstrating the value of the development, rather than on assessing the value of the cultural resource.

This distinction is at the heart of much of the current conflict concerning economic development both on and off today's Indian reservations. State and federal agencies are often unwilling to embrace the "avoidance first" perspective advocated by the tribes. In large part, this lack of agency willingness stems from the power of big business on government. In reality, the privately-owned electric utilities, road construction companies, logging interests, and mining operators—who almost invariably embrace a "mitigation first" perspective—are able to exert a large amount of influence on federal agencies whose programs run, in part, based on corporate tax dollars. Economist Richard Nafziger (1980) calls this pattern a symbiotic relationship between natural resource extraction (and other) companies and the federal government.

Nevertheless, there will be instances when the development is deemed necessary and of direct benefit to the tribe. In such cases, avoidance will still always be the first alternative. In those cases where avoidance is absolutely not possible, however, some difficult decisions must be made. This is particularly true when rapid economic development is a formal, explicit goal of the Navajo Nation government, in order to raise revenue for the general fund. Issues such as these are ones that clearly pit traditional and nontraditional forces against one another, making the existence of any common ground difficult to see for both sides, and making a win-win outcome more difficult to envision.

There is no easy way to make such difficult decisions regarding traditional cultural properties. Decisions regarding the lesser of two very close evils must be excruciating. In fact, one elder compared making such decisions to lining up his children and being forced to decide which ones not to shoot (Stoffle and Evans 1990, 95). The analogy with children being shot may at first sound overly dramatic, but for traditional people, the statement is accurate. Indeed, the individuals responsible for making such decisions experience the accompanying ethical conflict, grief, guilt, fear of reprisal, and emotional stress that would also accompany a decision concerning which children to let die. In this light, it may be easier to understand that if individuals or groups of individuals are willing to make such decisions, then the benefit had better greatly exceed the costs of the undertaking. The problem is also exacerbated by internal tribal conflicts and by the lack of trust that many traditional people have for the nontraditional bureaucrats who dominate the Navajo tribal government in Window Rock.

The alternative, however, may be that someone else decides which children will be shot. It is possible that in some cases this alternative may actually be preferred in order to shift the responsibility for such decisions to the shoulders of others (i.e., federal agencies). One group of anthropologists working in the field of traditional cultural properties has coined the phrase "cultural triage" for these kinds of forced-choice decisions (Stoffle and Evans 1990). The concept is based on medical triage, where medical professionals accept the general principle that all life is sacred, and work to maintain life at all costs. At times, however, medical professionals must also accept the reality that situational constraints force the selection of some patients to increase their chances of survival, while such decisions reduce the chance of survival for others. Common examples of medical triage include instances where war creates more wounded than there are treatment facilities, and where new medical advances such as artificial organs can save lives, but the demand is greater than the supply and some organ recipients have a better survival chance than others. Like medical triage, cultural triage may provide a framework to help tribes prioritize and rank traditional cultural properties such that the "more important ones" can be saved, and the "less important ones" can be sacrificed, for the greatest good for the greatest number.

Cultural triage is controversial within the realm of cultural resource management, particularly in regard to traditional cultural properties. Triage is common in an archaeological cultural resource management context, and the explicit ranking of sites reflects its acceptance. In such instances, however, the negative impact is felt almost exclusively by the scientific archaeological community, to whom mitigation through data recovery is a culturally acceptable alternative to avoidance. Since Indian communities do not generally share this philosophical perspective, however, it is highly problematic for anthropologists to ask them to willingly participate in the systematic ranking and subsequent slaughter of their own sacred properties. Such activity perpetuates the common Indian perception that anthropologists work to facilitate resource extraction by government and big business, rather than advocating for tribal concerns by pushing avoidance on the agencies. Given the inherent complexities of cultural triage work, the tribe must decide for itself whether they are willing to even entertain the idea of cultural triage, or whether they wish to stand with their more culturally compatible holistic conservation position that all the land is sacred and should not be disturbed.

In certain cases, the tribe may indeed wish to engage in cultural triage when they perceive that the economic benefit outweighs the cost. In other instances where the benefits do not clearly outweigh the costs, tribes may simply decide not to cooperate and remain with their complete avoidance stance.

Working with the Navajo Nation Archaeology Department

One example of land-altering federal undertaking that clearly outweighs the cultural costs is the closing of abandoned uranium mines. During the uranium boom of the 1940s and 1950s, the Cameron area, in the southwestern part of the reservation, produced the fourth largest amount of uranium in the state of Arizona (Scarborough 1981, 31–32). A total of 292,415 tons of uranium ore was mined from both deep pit and shallow surface mines in the region. With the rapid decrease in the demand for uranium beginning in the 1960s, the Cameron mines were abandoned; at least forty-five of them were left open and unused since that time. The open mines have caused many problems for the local residents. Small piles of pro-tore (low-grade uranium ore that was stockpiled for future use) is exposed to both wind and rain, creating hundreds of invisible radioactive "islands" interspersed throughout the residential and grazing land surrounding Cameron. The shallow surface mines often capture rainfall, creating standing pools where livestock drink and children swim. The runoff from the mines contains radioactive material that also contaminates groundwater supplies over large areas. In some instances, stone hogans were made out of uranium debris, some of which are still inhabited.[5]

Since the early 1990s, the Navajo Nation has been working to close these mines and reclaim the land. The Navajo Nation Abandoned Mine Lands Reclamation

Figure 6.1.   Author's photograph of abandoned uranium mine near Cameron, Arizona.

Department has set three priority levels for mine reclamation. First priority are shaft mines deeper than fifty feet, second priority are pits less than fifty feet, and third priority are surface uranium mines. First and second priority mines have largely been closed and reclaimed, and the third priority mines are in the process of having the necessary environmental and archaeological work done before they, too, can be closed and reclaimed. Shaft mine reclamation involves bulldozing the protore and tailings piles into the shafts, and topping the shafts with clean fill dirt brought in from elsewhere. Surface mines will be closed by first laying a plastic liner, bulldozing the protore and tailings piles onto the liner, laying down another plastic liner, and topping the liner with clean fill dirt. About 500 surface mines throughout the reservation currently remain open.

Everyone agrees that old uranium mines need to be closed. Due to the Surface Mining Control and Reclamation Act of 1977, however, mine closures are federal undertakings, thus triggering the Section 106 process. Additionally, most of the mines are at least fifty years of age, making them potentially eligible for the National Register. Prior to their closure and reclamation, archaeological and traditional cultural property surveys must be conducted. It is not unusual for abandoned mines to contain makeshift wooden or stone structures where people stayed and equipment was stored for short periods of time—these structures, and the extent of the mines themselves, need to be recorded. The Navajo Nation Archaeology Department has been contracted by the Abandoned Mine Lands Reclamation Program to carry out the cultural resource work and write the reports.

Although it is unlikely that the reservation's uranium mines will ever become photo opportunity tourist attractions, complete with snow globes and T-shirts, the mines are important for other reasons. Uranium mines need to be documented, evaluated, and perhaps listed on the National Register in part *because* of their infamy. If these mines had not been dug, the war in the Pacific may have had a different outcome, the nuclear weapons escalation of the Cold War may never have occurred, and a whole host of Navajo men may not have died of cancer. While it is true that in general, Anglo-owned companies prospected and operated the mines, the Navajo government organized the Navajo Prospector Program, which encouraged Navajos to prospect and operate their own mines. Indeed, the Cameron area was the most successful example of this program (Brugge, Benally, and Harrison 1997; e.g., Thompson and Anderson 1999 [NNAD Report No. 99–50]). Thus, the mines around Cameron are unique in a number of ways, and their physical and oral histories need to be recorded. For better or for worse, these mines are the physical expressions of an important era of our nation's past that has altered the lives of countless numbers of people, both locally and around the world. It is not necessary to be proud of our past to have the responsibility for managing it.

I meet Stephanie, an Anglo archaeologist working for the tribe, at Flagstaff's Navajo Nation Archaeology Department's office at eight o'clock in the morning. We load up the "tribie," a four wheel drive truck owned by the Navajo Nation's fleet of official government vehicles, and hit the road for a day of survey on the reservation. Isolated homes are scattered intermittently across the dry landscape. Simple dirt roads lead to the homes, really more a cluster of structures—a small frame house, a hogan or two, an outbuilding of rough-cut timber, an old trailer. Colorful medleys of vehicles in various states of inoperativeness dot the dirt yards. We pass Cameron, the site of a still-operating trading post, now functioning primarily for tourist sales. Only a small section towards the back stocks the everyday staples of interest to the surrounding Navajo families—bolts of cloth and velvet, iron skillets, huge sacks of Blue Bird Flour for making fry bread, and slabs of recently slaughtered mutton.

Today our work lies off the main road, to the north and west of Cameron; three uranium mines at the end of a dirt track are slated for reclamation. The mines vary greatly; the smallest is around one acre and the largest is around fifty acres, one is long and linear, while another is more of a square—all contain the characteristic debris piles of recently exposed, light-yellow-colored rock. First we survey the dirt road to the mines. Once the mines are reclaimed, the roads will be graded down with a bulldozer to discourage access, thus destroying any cultural resources along the roadsides. Upon project completion, the bulldozer will be given approval to scrape the dirt fifteen meters on both sides of the road—the right-of-way. I am responsible for finding anything cultural within my fifteen-meter swath. We carry little quivers full of bright orange pin flags to mark any artifacts we may find. We walk quickly, our eyes constantly combing the ground.

About twenty minutes into the survey, Stephanie spots a hogan ring. The only thing left of someone's old home is a circular pile of sandstone slabs measuring about four meters in diameter. Even without pulling out the compass we can tell which direction the hogan faced—east—as the sandstone slabs are unmistakably absent from the entryway. We survey the area around the hogan ring, flagging any debris associated with the hogan. We find a wood and iron object that looks like an old wagon part. We find several very old, rusty, crushed cans and old bottle glass from the 1950s. Near the hogan ring we see four smaller but discontinuous sandstone slabs that may have been the foundation for a small ramada—an outbuilding with a brush roof but no walls, which provided summertime shade for outdoor activities. Ramadas are still widely in use on the reservation today.

We record the site by mapping the hogan ring, the ramada foundation, and the location of the historic debris. We take photographs and compass bearings. We draw and describe the artifacts but do not collect them; the Navajo Nation wants all artifacts left in place. Nearby residents identify the hogan as belonging to one of their relatives, now deceased. Hogan rings are traditional cultural properties, as they were usually blessed before being lived in and most likely

Figure 6.2.   Author's photograph of old stone hogan ring found on survey.

witnessed numerous ceremonies during their occupation. As such, the physical remains of these abandoned homes may hold importance for living descendants. If the descendants decide they do not wish the hogan ring to be destroyed during the road closure, the site will be avoided.

The survey of the actual uranium mines—for obvious health reasons—is cursory. We walk a quick step around the mine perimeter, where engineers have pounded in stakes to mark the outer extent of land disturbance. We have been told not to eat or drink anything in the vicinity of the mines, as the ingestion of radioactive dust can be dangerous. Most mines contain nothing cultural, and we are able to leave quickly. One of the mines we surveyed, however, did contain a small sandstone structure with a wooden roof, now partially fallen in. An individual may have built this structure for refuge from the elements or as a place to store equipment. It is relatively un-usual to find a structure at a uranium mine; could it have been built by one of the independent Navajo prospectors that the tribe encouraged? We mapped and photographed the structure, and de-scribed it in detail on the site form. By recording the structure before it is destroyed we have at least partially documented some of the human behavior at this particular spot on the earth.

Traditional Cultural Property Interviews

In order to comply with the 1992 amendments to the National Historic Preser-vation Act, traditional cultural property interviews have become relatively standard practice, at least where significantly large Indian populations still reside. Since the mid-1990s, such interviews have accompanied cultural resource management work on the Navajo reservation.

Traditional cultural property interviews for projects such as water lines, electric lines, and uranium mine closures typically involve either an archaeologist or anthropologist working for the Archaeology Department, and ideally someone who speaks Navajo. The interviews usually consist of talking to the homeowners during door-to-door visits, and more formal chapter house interviews with local residents that correspond to the regular chapter meeting schedule (Ortiz 1999). Although important information may be gained, such is not always the case. For door-to-door interviews, it is often difficult to find anyone at home, and numerous repeat visits must be made. After many unsuccessful attempts to locate the residents, the interviewer may be forced to give up, and proceed with the project without their specific input. Conducting traditional cultural property interviews at the chapter house is not always successful either, as a quorum may not be present, and the meeting will be canceled. More traditional people may also not be willing to discuss specific personal sites, especially in a group setting, for confidentiality reasons discussed earlier.

Even when interviews are successful, the interviewer does not always gain relevant information. In a traditional cultural property survey near Coppermine, the majority of the responses were along the lines of (1) I married into the area, so I don't know what ceremonies occurred here or where; (2) I'm Christian, I don't care about such things; and (3) there's nothing important out there. Typically, such interviews are quite short, and reveal very little information. When reasonable attempts have been made to gather information concerning traditional cultural properties, the Archaeology Department must write a report of no significant findings, and allow the Historic Preservation Department to provide approval for the undertaking.

I meet Martha at the Flagstaff office of the Navajo Nation Archaeology Department. Martha, a Navajo woman and archaeology staff member in the Flagstaff office, has finished the archaeological survey and most of the traditional cultural property interviews for a domestic power line project. The project will bring much-desired power to approximately fifty dispersed Navajo homes. Families without electricity burn coal or wood, or buy gasoline-powered generators.

Not including the spur lines to individual homes, the power line itself will stretch many miles. Martha has walked this entire length twice—out and back—plus the spur lines. Today, she wants to return to one of the sites she found—a sweat lodge site—and take more photographs. When we arrive at the site, I can see numerous small depressions in the ground, each one about a meter across. Adjacent to each depression is a small pile of black, charcoal-stained dirt, full of reddish, fire-cracked rocks. These depressions and rock piles are the physical remains of sweat lodges. This was the long-term location of numerous purification ceremonies by Navajo men and women. Rocks would be heated in a fire outside of the lodge, and long wooden tongs would be used to move the rocks from the fire and place them in the center of the lodge. There, water would be poured over the hot rocks, and thick steam would fill the small space where several people would sit, chanting prayers of purification.

In her traditional cultural property interviews, no one had told Martha about the presence of old sweat lodges nearby. However, it is likely that many of the neighbors at least knew about the site. After Martha had found the site, she returned to the nearby homes and asked about the old sweat lodge area. The response was something like "yeah, the old folks used that area quite a bit for their sweats." It is not uncommon that once a traditional cultural property is found, only then are local residents willing to disclose more information about it. It is also likely that people would prefer not to discuss such issues publicly unless there is a need.

Perhaps some of the minimal disclosure concerning these kinds of traditional cultural properties stems from the fear that if they do request that a property be avoided, then their home may be dropped from the project or that the project will be delayed. Being dropped from the project means that the home will not get electricity or running water, and a delay may mean the project stalls indefinitely. Although homes are not dropped for such minor reroutes, despite assurances to the contrary, the fear still remains.

Minimal reporting of traditional cultural properties around the home may also stem from the possibility that local residents may no longer feel the need to give deference to the specific places where local ceremonies occurred. Rather, the belief now appears to be that once the ceremony has been completed and has had its effect, then the location itself loses special significance, despite the traditional belief that ceremonial locations mark the spot where supernatural power from the Holy People has been concentrated and absorbed (McPherson 1992a). Perhaps, given modern needs such as running water and electricity, this is one realm where allowances can be made, at least for individual, local ceremonies.

On the other hand, because such interviews generally result in a lack of interest for the avoidance of many traditional cultural properties near a home, when someone *does* request that a property be avoided, it means they truly wish for such an action to occur. In a sea of "don't worry about its," the infrequent "please leave that place alone" should be taken very seriously. At the very least, even when the outcome is minimal disclosure resulting in the destruction of traditional cultural properties, just asking people what they would like to have done with the properties shows a high level of respect for the people and the culture.

Notes

1. "Welfare Program in Tribal Hands," *Gallup Independent*, September 9, 2000.

2. For further information go to the Navajo Nation Historic Preservation Department, Navajo Nation Preservation Roads Planning Program, <http://hpd.navajo.org> (accessed February 25, 2002).

3. For further information go to the Navajo Nation Archaeology Department, <www.navajo.org/archaeology> (accessed February 26, 2002).

4. Through the Honoring Nations division of the American Indian Economic Development Program (with major funding by the Ford Foundation), Harvard showcases exemplary tribal programs that can be used as models for other tribes. For further information go to the Harvard Project on American Indian Economic Development, <http://ksgwww.harvard.edu/hpaied> (accessed February 25, 2002).

5. "Homes Near Old Mines Made of Uranium Bricks," *Gallup Independent*, November 13, 2000.

Traditional Cultural Properties: Scale, Benefits, and Broader Contexts

7

OR TRADITIONAL NAVAJO, all land is sacred. However, people can perceive land as sacred for different reasons and in different ways. This chapter looks at three broad kinds of traditional cultural properties: community scale, regional scale, and tribal scale. Anthropology's organizational methods seek to define cultural categories such as these with the ultimate goal of contrasting and comparing human societies worldwide. This chapter also discusses various pieces of legislation that go beyond the National Historic Preservation Act, but that nevertheless have bearing on the broader issue of traditional cultural properties. The discussion is also widened to bring in examples beyond the Navajo case study, to highlight the fact that such issues transcend any given tribe, and impact all of us.

Community Scale Traditional Cultural Properties

Extended family, various friends, and neighbors comprise the local Navajo community. Beyond the members of the immediate residential group, the local community is the group of individuals that interact most frequently. Such interaction often takes the form of reciprocal aid both in labor and in goods, as well as reciprocal attendance at important rites of passage—the milestones in the lives of known individuals. In addition to hogan rings and sweat lodges, community scale traditional cultural properties may include plant and mineral gathering places, burials, prayer offering areas, and shrines used by community members. These locations may also include the places where ceremonies were performed. Through the performance of ceremonies, the places themselves absorbed some of the power generated from the rituals designed to tap into the power of the Holy People. The longer a place was used for ceremonial purposes, the more power it absorbed. Even places that are now not used retain supernatural power. At the most minimal level, these locations may have witnessed important individuals' rites of passage that hold cultural significance at the personal level.

A *Kinaaldá* pit is another example of a traditional cultural property. A Kinaaldá is a Navajo girl's puberty ritual designed to announce and celebrate the onset of menstruation and to bless the girl as she enters womanhood. The ceremony involves the baking of a traditional cornmeal cake in an earth oven (see Frisbie 1967 for a complete description and analysis) that leaves an easily identifiable burned pit. The Kinaaldá is a very common ceremony among the Navajo today, although older women shake their heads at modern changes: "When *I* had *my* Kinaaldá, I had to grind the corn by hand; now they just go to the store and buy cornmeal *in bags!*" Extended family, neighbors, and various friends are all invited to attend the four-day ritual, which culminates with an all-night Blessingway ceremony for the young woman, conducted by a local medicine man. The entire ceremony is performed as a re-enactment of Changing Woman's Kinaaldá, first performed on Huerfano Mesa.

A friend invited me to her sister's Kinaaldá. Mary had just started her first menstruation the previous week. Family, friends and neighbors were quickly notified that the Kinaaldá would begin the following Thursday evening and would run through Monday morning. Throughout those four days guests were continually cycling through, bringing small gifts for Mary, and food contributions for the many meals that would be cooked for the guests. When

Figure 7.1.   Author's photograph of Kinaaldá pit found on survey.

I arrived, I offered to pitch in, and I was given the task of first washing dishes and then helping to make the next batch of mutton stew. Mary's father was digging the large (about one meter across), shallow hole in the ground where the Kinaaldá cornmeal cake would be baked. Various male relatives were chopping wood for the all-night fire over the earth oven. Mary, turquoise bedecked, was dressed in traditional women's attire with her hair partially pulled back and ritually tied with a strip of deerskin that had no wound holes from the kill. Eventually, we moved into the hogan, where Mary started sewing the cornhusk coverings for the cake. Mary had to sew the entire thing, working under her aunt's careful instructions. My role evolved into "official needle-threader." Mary began stirring the corn batter, mixed with hot water and copious amounts of raisins, using long greasewood sticks tied into a bundle. Quiet laughter filled the cozy hogan. Elder women directed the entire process.

When the batter was ready the lower corn husk covering was laid in the pit, the batter poured in, dry corn meal sprinkled on top in the four directions, and the upper corn husk covering laid overtop. Earth was shoveled on and a fire built over top, which burned all night. Late into the evening a medicine man arrived, and sang the Blessingway all night. At dawn, we all ran out of the hogan toward the east, to help ensure that Mary would not be a lazy woman. Mary was later "molded" by an elder woman of high regard so that she would become a woman of high regard herself. Mary then "stretched" the guests—including me—to make sure we would grow strong and tall. Minimally suppressed giggles accompanied the lighthearted ritual. We cut the huge cake out of the earth oven, chunk by chunk, and feasted. Only Mary could not eat her cake, so that she would always be generous to others. The Kinaaldá pit—the edges charred a dark red—was left open as a physical manifestation of Mary's womanhood.

The Indian Health Service (IHS) is responsible for providing healthcare on Indian reservations. As part of a larger public health initiative, IHS is in the process of running water lines to private homes and in building septic systems for human waste. Since the IHS is a federal agency, the construction of water lines and septic systems is a federal undertaking, and hence, by law, traditional cultural property interviews must be completed prior to the land-altering improvements.

As part of my work at the Navajo Nation Archaeology Department, I participated in a water line survey in the Smith Lake chapter. I worked with Mike, a young Navajo man employed as an archaeologist with the Navajo Nation Archaeology Department. Although the home where I attended the Kinaaldá, for example, was not far from the main paved road, there was no running water. Rainwater off the roof was caught in barrels and biweekly treks were made by pickup truck to an IHS tank to bring water back home to store in the barrels. We heated water for dishwashing and bathing, and an outhouse stood to the far side of the sheep corral. Through the IHS , life is not only being made easier for the Navajo people, but disease transmission is being reduced.

The water line survey involved numerous stages. First, Mike and I met with the IHS engineer who had staked out the pathway of the proposed line. We drove the route with the engineer, an Anglo woman from Texas. She pointed out the twenty-four homes that were slated to get running water and septic systems and the route the line would take between the widely scattered homes. Over the next two weeks we walked the land around each of the twenty-four homes. We were required to walk a 200-foot swath around each home so that the septic system could be built somewhere within that radius. The water line itself required a 100-foot survey on both sides of the line to allow for bulldozer and truck access during both the construction and maintenance of the line.

Our arrival at the homes was always well announced by a chorus of barking dogs. If the homeowner was not present, we kept our eyes peeled for the nearest throwing stone in case the dogs did not prove friendly. Many of the residents we spoke with asked when they would actually get water. Mike didn't know for sure, but he thought it would take about three years. Although some people took this news with great dignity, others were obviously exasperated. Application for water services begins at the local chapter house. The process moves forward when enough people serviceable from a given line have applied, and when the chapter has pulled together a written proposal to pass along to the tribal government's Division of Health. Once the Division of Health has prioritized its list for water service, the ranking is passed on to IHS . Clearly, the process of getting running water on the reservation is a very long one.

Given the length of the process, it is probably not too surprising that not a single home out of the twenty-four surveyed at Smith Lake expressed concern about traditional cultural properties, despite the fact that we found several such properties in our survey. One of the homes in Smith Lake had a Kinaaldá pit near one of the hogans. The Kinaaldá had taken place quite recently, performed for the granddaughter of the woman who was to receive running water. A Kinaaldá pit is an example of a community-scale traditional cultural property, as it commemorates an important event not only in the life of one individual girl, but as an important event in the lives of the community. In former times a Kinaaldá ceremony served as a formal announcement to the local community that this girl was now eligible for marriage. In former times, most girls were married within about a year of their Kinaaldá (Frisbie 1967).

The grandmother who owned the property where the Kinaaldá pit stood as a proud monument to her granddaughter's womanhood, was not at home for our traditional cultural property interview. We asked around, and since everyone knew about the recent Kinaaldá, it was not difficult to locate the family where the young woman resided. We spoke with her father regarding the Kinaaldá pit. We needed to know what should be done with it: should it be avoided when the water line and septic system were built, or was it alright to destroy it if that ended up being the most suitable location for the septic tank? The father did not see any reason the

Kinaaldá pit could not be destroyed, but he felt it would be necessary to discuss the issue with his mother, who was currently out of town. We would need to return for the answer.

The next week we returned to find the Kinaaldá pit had been filled in with dirt and the surrounding ground was smoothed over as if nothing unusual had occurred at that location. To make sure this action indeed meant that the Kinaaldá pit did not need to be mapped, recorded, and avoided, we again spoke with the father. He confirmed our assessment: the Kinaaldá pit did not need to be saved.

Regional Scale Traditional Cultural Properties

A regional scale traditional cultural property is important to a group of people beyond a local community. In fact, individuals to whom a regional scale traditional cultural property is important may not even know each other. Rather than the locations of specific ceremonies performed within the lifetimes of individuals, regional scale traditional cultural properties tend to be important landforms, or have been the long-term location of a variety of ceremonies. These properties are usually named locations, although neither the name nor the place itself is likely to be known beyond the immediate region.

One such place on the Navajo Reservation is Little Black Spot Mountain. Little Black Spot Mountain—*Dził Dah Zhin*—is a steep-sided mesa near Piñon, Arizona

Figure 7.2. Author's photograph of Little Black Spot Mountain, near Piñon, Arizona.

(Linford 2000, 105). As a high spot on the horizon (elevation 7,000 feet), people living in several surrounding communities can see it. As part of a broader goal of improving communications, it was proposed that a microwave tower be built on the top of Little Black Spot Mountain. An electrical power line was also to be located there, and as part of the construction and maintenance of the tower an access road would need to be built to the top of the mountain. The Navajo Tribal Utility Authority (NTUA) is a tribal government enterprise funded by grants from the Rural Utilities Service of the federal Department of Agriculture. Thus, as the sponsor of the microwave tower and rural electrification undertaking, the (NTUA) action triggered the Section 106 process.

Traditional cultural property interviews with area residents were conducted through the Navajo Nation Archaeology Department and were geared specifically toward Little Black Spot Mountain. As revealed in the interviews, the mountain was important for many reasons (Dalgai 1995). First, an Anasazi archaeological site graced its summit. Secondly, it was an important place for the gathering of medicinal and ceremonial plants such as wide and narrow leaf yucca, juniper, fir, willow, gamble oak, snakeweed, cliffrose, squirreltail, and greasewood. Thirdly, as a local concentration of supernatural power, many ceremonies had been performed there over the years. Numerous Enemyway (see figures 7.3 and 7.4 for additional examples of community scale traditional cultural properties) ceremonies have been performed there since the 1930s and continue to be performed at this

Figure 7.3.   Author's photograph of temporary structure used for cooking and socializing during an Enemyway ceremony.

Figure 7.4.   Author's photograph of temporary brush hogan used during an Enemyway ceremony.

site today. In 1930 a Yei-bi-chei was performed there, and in 1990 a number of local residents remembered that a Fire Dance[1] also occurred there. Many sweat lodges, both old and recent, dotted the mesa's sides. There was a game trap from the 1800s that could still be seen, and numerous historic Navajo burials were said to be there. Prayer offerings and stone shrines occurred at several locations. And finally, in 1956, a widow had built a juniper brush structure on the mountain for Christian prayer services for her then recently deceased husband.

Clearly, Little Black Spot Mountain was very important to many area residents and had been a major focal point for a wide variety of ceremonial activities by many individuals over a long period of time. The individuals may or may not have known one another and may or may not have been present at the various rituals. It was, however, a clear consensus by area residents that it would not be appropriate to simply ignore the importance of the location and go ahead with the construction. Through consultation with the Navajo Nation Historic Preservation Department, a mitigation plan was developed and agreed upon by all parties. The mitigation plan included three primary measures.

First, the NTUA would pay for a medicine man to perform a Blessingway ceremony both before and after the project completion. The Blessingway would communicate the lack of bad intentions to the supernatural beings associated with Little Black Spot Mountain. Secondly, new road construction would be minimal and the existing road and utility poles would be used whenever possible. Thirdly, the NTUA would install a gate at the base of the mountain so as to limit access and discourage casual use of the mountain. Finally, the Anasazi site atop the mountain would be avoided. With these mitigation measures assured, the Historic Preservation Department provided project approval to the NTUA, and the construction proceeded. Both the individual community scale traditional cultural properties on Little Black Spot Mountain were avoided and the overall integrity of the mountain itself, a regional scale traditional cultural property, was maintained.

Tribal Scale Traditional Cultural Properties

Rising more than a mile above the surrounding grasslands, the San Francisco Peaks are a prominent feature of the southern Colorado Plateau. On clear days, the Peaks are visible from more than a hundred miles away. Due perhaps to their visibility on the horizon, many Indian tribes in the Southwest consider the Peaks to be a sacred site—a traditional cultural property. To the Navajo, the San Francisco Peaks are known as Dook'o'oosłííd (Never Thaws on Top) (See chapter 3, Linford 2000, 128; Van Valkenburgh 1974, 105).

As the westernmost of the four sacred mountains, the San Francisco Peaks are an important foundation of the Navajo universe. The Navajo Nation flag, as well as the Great Seal of the Navajo Nation, have the four sacred mountains as readily identifiable, prominent symbols that help define Navajo culture. Most Navajo, even nontraditional ones, can easily rattle off the names of the four sacred mountains. Numerous shrines, offering places, and plant and mineral gathering areas exist throughout the Peaks. Although community scale ceremonies may be performed there and the Peaks may be regionally important for those Navajo living nearby, they are mostly recognized for their importance at the tribal scale. Tribal scale traditional cultural properties typically are major landforms and almost always are individually named. These named places symbolize the land and culture of the Navajo as a whole, and figure prominently in Navajo origin stories. The Blessingway, the most common Navajo ceremony to confer protection, harmony, and good fortune, recounts the creation of the four sacred mountains by the Holy People (Wyman 1970).

As is the case with the three other sacred mountains, the San Francisco Peaks do not sit on Navajo Reservation Land. Instead, the Peaks are public lands administered through the United States Forest Service, Coconino National Forest, and the Peaks Ranger District—a federal agency. As clearly defined through the Navajo Land Claims, however, the San Francisco Peaks are a part of the Navajo's traditional use area, and as such the Navajo must be consulted prior to land-altering development.

The biggest and most controversial development in the Peaks has been a downhill ski resort, the Arizona Snowbowl. The first ski lodge in the Peaks was built in 1938, when the Flagstaff Ski Club acquired the original federal permit. The original lodge burned in 1952 and was rebuilt further up slope in 1956, and a single rope tow was used to pull people to the top of the existing slopes. Chairlifts were installed in 1958 and 1962 as additional ski slopes were cut out of the heavy ponderosa pine forests. Since 1962, only very minor changes have occurred to the Snowbowl facilities, even though skiers were beginning to crowd the slopes, and an inevitable upgrade and expansion in facilities was becoming apparent.

Beginning in the mid-1970s, with the demand for enhanced ski facilities reaching a fever pitch, the private company operating the Snowbowl petitioned the Forest Service to allow facility enhancement. The original 1938 federal permit for the Snowbowl specified the maximum level of ski facility development that would be allowed. Although the enhanced ski facilities proposed in the 1970s did not exceed this maximum, the many people interpreted these enhancements as unwanted expansion. Certainly there was much support for enhanced facilities by ski enthusiasts, but there were a number of other groups not so keen on the idea of more development in the San Francisco Peaks.

When the original permit was granted to Snowbowl developers in 1938, there were fewer federal requirements to assess the negative impacts of development on federal land. By the late 1970s, however, quite a bit of pertinent federal legislation had been passed. The Endangered Species Act and the National Environmental Policy Act had been passed, both designed to consider and in some cases actually protect endangered flora and fauna. And of course, the National Historic Preservation Act of 1966 and the American Indian Religious Freedom Act of 1978 had also been signed into law since the original 1938 Snowbowl permit. Thus, the Forest Service was required to write an Environmental Impact Statement[2] prior to approving the Snowbowl enhancements. Such a document was published in 1979, outlining alternative developments and stating the specific negative impacts to various resources for each alternative.

Unlike the United States Forest Service, the National Park Service oversees land that is specifically set aside for environmental preservation and allows minimal impact recreation activities. No logging or mining or other land-altering development is permitted. The Forest Service's mandate, however, is quite different and is summarized in their slogan "Land of Many Uses." While sounding good in theory, in reality this multiple use strategy can be difficult to juggle, as many interest groups compete for the same land base. Multiple use involves managing a variety of resource needs including outdoor recreation, rangeland for grazing, timber and mineral extraction, watershed concerns, fish and wildlife, and biological and cultural resources. The Forest Service is the land manager for the San Francisco Peaks and is responsible for making decisions that best meet the demands of all parties. At the same time, however, the Forest Service remains accountable by law for the responsible stewardship of the varied resources they are mandated to manage.

In the Forest Service's 1979 Environmental Impact Statement, the interested parties are listed as:

1. The Flagstaff Business Community
   Hotels, restaurants, bars, gas stations, and other services benefit from the Snowbowl. The Northern Arizona University School of Business estimates that each skier contributes $23.25 (in 1979 dollars) per day to the local economy (Final Environmental Impact Statement 1979, 65). With an average of 101 ski days a year, and the pre-enhancement rate of 1,065 skiers per day, a total of $2.5 million is pumped into the Flagstaff economy each year. The approved enhancements would increase slope capacity to accommodate 3,430 skiers, boosting area businesses up to $7 million. This economic contribution also occurs during the winter season, when fewer people pass through Flagstaff on their way to the Grand Canyon, the major summertime tourist draw.

2. The State of Arizona Skiers
   Limited ski opportunities exist for Arizonans, and an un-enhanced Snowbowl is not attractive for beginners. The proposed enhancements would provide a more even distribution of slopes to meet the skill level of a wider variety of skiers. If ski slope capacity expands, however, so too must the chairlift capacity, or else people would wait an unacceptable length of time to ride back to the top. Lodge and parking facilities must also expand and the access road must be widened, all of which disturb the land.

3. The Southwestern Indian Tribes
   Although other tribes have religious concerns regarding the San Francisco Peaks, the Navajo and the Hopi by far voiced the largest concern over any existing and all new development in the San Francisco Peaks. (As was made clear in the 1999 changes to 36 CFR 800—the implementing regulations of the National Historic Preservation Act—Native American tribes have compelling reasons to be given a more prominent role in negotiations than other interested parties [Federal Register Vol. 64, No. 95]. These reasons include sovereignty, a direct government to government relationship, trust status, and treaty rights. In the 1970s, however, the enhanced role of Indian tribes in federal negotiations had not yet been established.)

4. The General Public
   In the public comments and meetings period, no single consensus opinion could be identified. In general, there was much concern voiced about protecting Native American beliefs.

When the effects of a federal undertaking are considered through an Environmental Impact Statement, the federal agency—in this instance the Forest Service—has the authority to make the final decision regarding the undertaking. Such a final decision can only be made, however, after demonstrating a good faith effort to consult and negotiate with all affected parties, including Indian tribes. For a decision to stand, an agency must be prepared to show in a court of law that indeed a good faith effort was made. Throughout the 1970s, it was clear that the Navajo and Hopi were in strong opposition to the proposed Snowbowl enhancements—and certainly to any expansion beyond permit limits. Contained in the 1979 report are numerous letters of opposition from Indian tribes, clearly stating their complete lack of support for the Forest Service's preferred alternative regarding the Snowbowl. Various individual Hopi villages and Navajo chapters wrote letters, and a detailed statement was sent by then-Navajo Tribal Chairman Peter MacDonald (Final EIS, 236–38). Even the BIA sent a letter stating that they support the formal position taken by the Navajo tribe.

Also in the mid-1970s, the Snowbowl owners applied for a completely new special use permit. This permit requested Forest Service permission to build condominiums and a golf course in a nearby area known as Hart's Prairie, and to link the area with the Snowbowl by chairlift. Intense public pressure followed. The Forest Service denied the permit, stating that any development beyond that specified by the original federal permit would not be allowed. The condominium and golf complex was not built.

In 1979 the Forest Service approved the Snowbowl enhancements. These enhancements included the construction of a new lodge, the reconstruction of the existing chairlift, the construction of three new lifts, the development of a portable chairlift for use above tree line, the expansion of parking lots, and the construction of fifty acres of new ski runs (Van Otten 1982, 2). Due to public pressure, these approved enhancements still have not been carried out. A very large part of that public pressure was in the form of a lawsuit under the American Indian Religious Freedom Act, brought by the Hopi, Zuni, and Navajo tribes.

The American Indian Religious Freedom Act And Broader Traditional Cultural Properties Issues

Passed in 1978, the American Indian Religious Freedom Act seeks "to protect and preserve for American Indians their inherent right of freedom to believe, express, and exercise the traditional religions . . . including but not limited to access to sites, use and possession of sacred objects, and the freedom to worship through ceremonials and traditional rites" (AIRFA Public Law 95-341). In part, the act was spurred on by both open immigration and drug enforcement concerns: Indians traveling to and from Canada and Mexico would carry prayer bags that contained religious items, including peyote for ritual use during Native American Church meetings—the Indians would be questioned and at times harassed by the drug enforcement agents due to the contents of their prayer bags (AIRFA Federal Agencies Task Force Report, 1979).

The lawsuit, under the American Indian Religious Freedom Act brought by the Hopi, Zuni, and Navajo tribes, contested the Forest Service's decision on the Arizona Snowbowl. In 1980, a judge ruled against the tribes, stating that the Act does not require that Indians be granted exclusive access to public lands without consideration for other uses or activities, nor does it require that native religious practices should prevail to the exclusion of all other interests and concerns. Although the tribes appealed the decision to higher courts, there has yet to be a ruling in the tribes' favor.

The San Francisco Peaks Arizona Snowbowl suit was the first legal interpretation of the American Indian Religious Freedom Act. There were a number of important outcomes of the failed suit. First, the court decision makes clear that American Indians are indeed guaranteed protection under the First Amendment of the Constitution,[3] but that they are not granted any rights above and beyond that guarantee. Secondly, it became clear that although federal agencies are now required to consult with Indian tribes regarding access and impacts to their religious sites, the Act does not provide guidelines or regulations as to how the consultation will actually proceed. As a result, the American Indian Religious Freedom Act is very unlike the National Historic Preservation Act because it does not specify the rights, responsibilities, and obligations of each of the parties involved. Rather, the Act constitutes only a broad policy statement with limited practical utility on a day-to-day basis. Thus, at present, the American Indian Religious Freedom Act is a relatively weak piece of legislation for both Indians and for the federal agencies that manage traditional cultural properties.

Even though the 1980 court decision ruled against the tribes, it also reinforced the need to consult with them. Executive Order 13084, signed by President Clinton in 1998, directly addresses the issue of Indian consultation. Coming almost twenty years after the court decision on the Snowbowl, this order clarifies that tribal representatives have the right to regular and meaningful consultation. Not surprisingly, however, consultation means different things to different people (Federal Register 64, No. 95). To tribes, consultation is understood to mean working toward a consensus and thus is closely akin to negotiation. Consulting parties—tribes in particular—have an impact on not only the decision making process, but on the actual outcome as well. For the agencies, consultation has often meant that if the tribe has been contacted, attended the meetings, and had the opportunity to express their views on the issue, then the tribe has been consulted, regardless of the actual outcome. What has become very clear to tribes, once the 1992 National Historic Preservation Act amendments were implemented, is that notification is not consultation (Downer 2000). Ultimately, however, the federal agency must make the final decision regarding an outcome. They must also be able to prove that they made a good faith effort to consult with the tribe.

Executive Order 13007, written in 1996 and also signed by President Clinton, addresses the protection of sacred sites. This order requires federal agencies to accommodate ceremonial access to sacred sites, avoid adversely impacting such sites, and maintain confidentiality concerning the location of these sites from the general public. These executive orders and 1994 amendments to the American Indian Religious Freedom Act are all designed to strengthen Indian religious rights to the land. They seem, however, to be willing to do so only when other compelling interests are not also at stake. In reality, this is rarely the case.

The 1980 court decision against the tribes also reiterated and supported the Forest Service policy of multiple use. Snowbowl supporters have argued that since the Snowbowl is located on the western side of the Peaks and thus is invisible from both the Hopi and Navajo Reservations, the ski area's impact is lessened for the tribe. The Snowbowl enhancements do not prohibit Indian people from entering the area and collecting plants or minerals for use in ceremonies, nor does it prohibit offerings and ceremonies in the permit area. Snowbowl supporters also argue that the ski area occupies around 1 percent of the land considered as the San Francisco Peaks, and the vast majority of the land in the Peaks Ranger District remains largely as wilderness. These areas have always been and continue to be open for traditional ceremonial use.

> The fairness of the multiple use doctrine has been stated through the years. The fairness of using part of an area to do one thing and part of an area to do another is obvious. We are talking about Forest Service lands. These are our lands. They belong to the people of the United States of America, including Hopi and Navajo [and Zuni]. We have in this country a polyglot of people who all have their specific interests. They've been brought together in a unified nation. Public lands are for all of us to use for some measure of pleasure and peace. This includes recreationists, ranchers, photographers, lovers, atheists, and the sincerely religious. No one set of rights prevails (Van Otten 1982, 22).[4]

Although the court ruling seems at first glance to be fair, it misses something basic in the understanding of native religions. Navajo religion, like many nonindustrial societies, is land-based, in that it is anchored to specific landscapes. Spider Woman lives at Spider Rock, and *that* is where rituals must be performed for her, at specific shrines that have been used for centuries. There is not an option to do those particular ceremonies elsewhere. Likewise, Navajo healing rituals work only within the confines of the four sacred mountains. Elsewhere, those very same rituals are ineffective. Not all traditional Navajo religious practice is tethered to the land in such a way, however. Community scale religious practices can be performed in any setting, or at least any setting within the four sacred mountains. But practices tied to regional and tribal scale traditional cultural properties, however, are different in the fact that they do need to be performed in certain, specific locations. Modern intrusions, such as camera-toting tourists, loud music blaring from a ski lodge, and cars whizzing by on the road to the lodge, make the practice of land-based, place-specific religion unpalatable, and hence its continuity is threatened.

As such, the practice of at least some aspects of traditional Navajo religion is fundamentally incompatible with modern land use practices as articulated by the Forest Service's multiple use policy. What the judges have ruled as granting religious rights in excess of other interests in some ways is like comparing apples and oranges. The land needs of different religious perspectives are themselves different. Some religions are relatively mobile, whereas others are not. Although Christianity originated in the Middle East, it can easily be transported and practiced anywhere. Navajo religion cannot be practiced anywhere. It may work for Christians and nontraditional Navajo to place offerings at a new shrine on the other side of the mountain, but for Navajo belief it is not necessarily always that simple. Just as Navajo medicine men are generally not permitted to add personal variations to their rituals, one is not at liberty to move the location of a shrine or offering place simply because others want to ski down the mountain.

I drive the winding road up the San Francisco Peaks, on my way to the Arizona Snowbowl. Beautiful stands of huge aspen line the narrow roadside, their gleaming white trunks stark and surprising against the deep greens of summertime and the bright, cobalt blue sky. I pass the wooden Forest Service sign proclaiming their jurisdiction over this piece of ancient land. I wanted to experience for myself the infamous site of the ski resort built on the sacred mountain of the west. I see the first ski slopes cut through the forest, and I pull over to take some pictures, somehow feeling like I'm doing a photo-documentary of a massacre in Bosnia. I half expect to see Satan himself appear before my eyes, swinging his legs from the chairlift passing overhead. Instead, I see hikers eating lunch at the picnic tables, relaxing in the warmth of the summer sunshine. We listen to the radio music coming from a loudspeaker attached to the wall of the small lodge. A blackboard announces a BLT special for lunch. It all seems so normal.

Friends have told me that they don't like skiing at the Snowbowl because the services are inadequate and facilities run down. Other friends have told me that they won't even go to the Snowbowl because of its desecrating infamy. Forest Service personnel have told me that while the San Francisco Peaks are not actually on the National Register, they are managing them as if they were. Indeed, the White Vulcan Mine, where pumice stone was mined from the Peaks to make stone washed jeans, was recently shut down with great celebration and hoopla, with the federal government providing financial compensation to the mine owners. Visiting this place brings home for me the difficulty of negotiating over traditional cultural properties and economic development. Much like democracy itself, the process of managing traditional cultural properties is imperfect. While great in theory, in practice it is just plain hard, particularly in high-profile tourist areas, and particularly regarding high-profile tribal scale traditional cultural properties. In such instances, both federal land managers and tribal representatives are put in the unenviable position of making very difficult decisions that are sure to not please everyone, or else they become entrenched, wedded to their particular perspective, and unwilling to budge. It is at places like the San Francisco Peaks where rubber literally and figuratively hits the road, and the spirit as well as the letter of the law is put to the test.

Traditional Cultural Properties beyond Navajoland

This section broadens the discussion to include the traditional cultural properties of other native peoples—a Zuni example in the Southwest, two Northern Plains examples, and even further afield to an Australian example. Indeed, many such global examples could be cited, particularly numerous in those countries where relatively recent European colonization has created a dominant society, with indigenous, native groups as minorities. All of these examples involve tribal scale traditional cultural properties, and in some cases these properties could even be considered as pan-tribal in many ways. Thus, although this book has used the Navajo as the vehicle to discuss traditional cultural properties, the issue itself reaches far beyond Navajoland (see Gulliford 2000 for discussions of numerous traditional cultural properties in the United States).

Zuni Ceremonial Location, New Mexico

The Zuni are a Puebloan group whose primary reservation land is a small area in west central New Mexico. Today, the tribe's 8000 or so tribal members live mostly in one main pueblo. During certain times of the year, Zuni kachina dancers—masked and adorned in ritual attire—dance in various of the pueblo's plazas to honor the kachina spirits that bring rain and good fortune to the people. By the early 1990s, however, it had become clear that the Zuni needed a new sewer line. The Environmental Protection Agency—a federal agency initiating a federal undertaking—suggested installing a gravity-based sewer line through the pueblo. If gravity was to run the system, there were a limited number of routes the line could take. Unfortunately, the line's path was to go directly through one of the ceremonial locations used by the kachina dancers prior to their plaza dances (Avallone, Othole, and Anyon 1992).

When the Zuni were first approached about the possibility of tearing up their ceremonial location to run the line, they were not at all interested, and by law they had the right to halt the project on their own land due to tribal sovereignty. However, during continued discussions it became clear that the problem did not in fact center on the actual location of the construction. Rather, the Zuni were much more concerned that the construction would interfere with their ceremonies and dances that occurred based on a ritual calendar, itself aligned with the seasons. At least for the Zuni and at least in this instance, during specific times of the year certain places have great significance, but during the rest of the year, they don't. Thus, the mitigation measures ended up actually being quite simple to negotiate: sewer construction would need to occur during seasons when these location-specific ceremonial activities were not taking place, and the impacted area needed to be returned to its proper, pre-construction condition by the time the ceremonies were due to commence. A unique and creative solution was found—through genuine discussion and negotiation—that enabled a win-win outcome for everyone concerned. This example highlights the point that there is an important temporal dimension to traditional cultural properties, and as long as the timing of the undertaking is flexible, scheduling may be the easiest of all mitigation measures to adopt (see Brock 1989 for a discussion of gender dimensions of traditional cultural properties).

Devils Tower / Bear Lodge, Wyoming

Moving to the Northern Plains of North America, the case of Devils Tower National Monument in Wyoming is also relevant. Devils Tower was America's first national monument, and it was established to protect the huge basalt obelisk with fluted sides[5] that has become exceedingly popular with rock climbers (Dussias 1999). Eligible for inclusion as a traditional cultural property in the National Register of Historic Places, many Northern Plains Indian groups refer to Devils Tower as Bear Lodge. This name comes from oral traditions concerning its creation: Some children took refuge on a rock [or a tree stump] from a bear, which was chasing them. Upon praying for help, the rock [or tree stump] rose far into the air, taking the children well out of the bear's reach. The bear clawed at the rock [or tree stump], causing the many vertical grooves in the huge monolith. Now safe, the children turned into important star constellations and the rock [or tree stump] turned into Bear Lodge. Vision quests, purification sweats in sweat lodges, prayer offerings, ceremonial plant gathering, and the performance of Sun Dances all occur at Bear Lodge.

Although the Tower has been climbed for recreation for over a hundred years, the last few decades have seen an explosion in both the numbers of climbers and in the number of routes established. In 1973 there were only 312 climbers and fifty-one routes to the summit; as of the late 1990s there are over 6,000 climbers annually and at least 220 named routes that traverse even the most remote areas of the Tower. Poorly managed climbing also damages resources mandated by law to be protected by the National Park Service. As of 1992, there were 580 bolts and several hundred pitons permanently placed in the Tower, numerous chalk markings, and webbing and ropes left in place for future climbs littered the Tower. Numerous prairie falcon nesting sites have also been disturbed. Due to the fact that climbers could pop up almost anywhere at anytime, it had become increasingly difficult to find privacy for the practice of traditional native ceremonies.

After the Lakota, Nakota, and Dakota submitted a formal resolution concerning the out-of-control climbing situation, the National Park Service, with input from all affected interest groups, formulated a number of climbing regulations (Dussias 1999). These regulations attempted to balance the desires of those groups that had been favored in the past—the climbers—and the cultural uses of Native Americans, which historically had received little respect. The climbing plan also attempted to protect the locations of nesting raptors. The regulations included a voluntary climbing ban for the month of June to correspond with summer solstice ceremonial activities, the prohibition of adding new bolts and pitons, the replacement of existing ropes and webbing with camouflaged equipment, and a fifty-meter buffer zone around falcon nests. The Park Service has also implemented a cross-cultural education program to promote public understanding of the issue. A name change may also be in the works. Although not all climbers have observed the voluntary June climbing ban, most have. Various lawsuits are pending, however, as brought forward primarily by the commercial climbing operations.

Bighorn Medicine Wheel, Wyoming

Another well-known example of a traditional cultural property whose management has generated controversy also comes from the Northern Plains—the Bighorn Medicine Wheel in Wyoming (Bighorn National Forest brochure; Gill 1982; Price 1994). Medicine wheels are not natural landforms, but rather are rock features built in the shape of wagon wheels and can be found in many areas of the Northern Plains. Alberta, Canada has the largest concentration of these features with a total of forty-six wheels, constituting about three-quarters of all known wheels. The Bighorn Medicine Wheel[6]—the southernmost known wheel—measures about eighty feet across and consists of twenty-eight spokes radiating out of a central rock cairn. Six additional rock cairns are spaced along the rim of the wheel with four of the cairns lining up with the rising and setting sun of the summer solstice. Archaeological evidence suggests the wheel was built between 1200 and 1700 A.D., before the historic Plains Indians occupied the region. Historically, the Crow Indians, among others, used the wheel as part of vision quest ceremonies and left prayer offerings. Chief Joseph of the Nez Percé is known to have visited the wheel to pray for wisdom in leading his people in the transition from freedom to reservation life. New Age practitioners have also recently adopted the Bighorn Medicine Wheel as an important pilgrimage place, and many, many thousands of people visit the wheel each summer.

The Bighorn Medicine Wheel is located on land managed by the Bighorn National Forest—a federal agency. In 1993, the Forest Service began to carry out a plan agreed upon through consultation brought about through the implementation of the National Historic Preservation Act's Section 106 (Salerno 1993). Based on these consultations, certain regulations are now in place. Vehicle access to the wheel is allowed only for handicapped and elderly individuals, while the rest of the visitors hike the one and a half mile trail. Specially trained interpreters work at the site. A wire fence was constructed around the wheel to prevent theft (souvenir-taking) and unintentional damage. The wheel is also off limits to non-Native American practitioners for three days around each solstice and equinox, and for twelve other days during the year to allow for uninterrupted ceremonial activities. The plan also incorporates Indian people into the Bighorn National Forest's Advisory Board. An ongoing issue that continues to generate controversy is the definition of boundaries. The Forest Service, snowmobilers, and timber and mining companies would like to place the wheel's boundaries near the edge of the wheel itself—a piecemeal approach—whereas others would like all of Medicine Mountain, upon which the wheel rests, declared part of the traditional cultural property—a landscape approach.

Uluru/Ayer's Rock, Australia

The United States is not the only country grappling with ways to bring together development and the needs of traditional, land-based religion (Tarlock 1999). Australian Aborigines in central Australia have long held Uluru (formerly called Ayers Rock, after a previous Prime Minister) as sacred (Cowan 1992; Ritchie 1994). This huge, rounded, red sandstone monolith emerges abruptly from the surrounding landscape, towering a thousand feet high and stretching over several miles.[7] At sunset, Uluru glows bright red. The rock itself is understood to represent a rising up in grief after a hideous, Dreaming-era slaughter between two angry tribes. Aborigine tradition also holds that Uluru is one of several major supernatural power nodes. These nodes connect and provide "current" to long lines that run across the landscape. The location and meaning of the landforms encountered in these lines—the physical markings left by the Dreaming spirits—are ritually embedded in song. Singing these songs connects the singer to the Dreaming spirits.

After some two hundred years of Anglo-Australian control, Uluru was formally returned to local Aboriginal ownership in 1985 (De Lacy and Lawson 1997; see also Ritchie 1994). An Aborigine Board and the Australian Federal Government jointly manage the National Park that surrounds the rock. Part of the management agreement is that the Aboriginal owners lease the land to the federal government for an annual fee and for a 25 percent share of park proceeds. The economic value of tourism is being partially captured by hotel, restaurant, and cultural tourism programs owned and run by Aboriginal people. Park visitors are expected to abide by certain restrictions. Several areas are entirely closed, and one established hiking trail is the only access allowed to the top of Uluru— although technically not off limits, visitors are discouraged from hiking on the rock itself. Through interpretive programs the Park educates visitors regarding reasons for the restrictions, in part to overcome negative reactions but also to actively foster the concept that the park is a living cultural landscape.

Devils Tower, the Bighorn Medicine Wheel, and the Zuni sewer line are all examples of the National Historic Preservation Act at work. The case of Uluru, Australia, while similar in many ways, involved the actual and complete transfer of legal ownership of the property in question, despite the fact that tourism is Australia's fastest growth industry. Without doubt, there are individuals and groups on both sides of these particular issues. Some clearly feel the compromises and accommodations have not gone far enough and that federal agencies negotiate with half a heart at best, and even then only because they have to. Other groups and individuals feel that these accommodations and compromises have gone way too far, with their constitutional rights being trampled upon. Although the goal of the National Historic Preservation Act is to produce a win-win outcome, this is not always going to happen for all concerned. Legal battles rage on both sides, with the federal agency beholden to prove to all sides that they made a good faith effort to consult and negotiate for the desires of all parties. The process can be slow and tedious and is far from perfect, and not everyone will be happy all the time. For the moment, however, it is the best approach we have.

Boiled down to its most elemental form, a deeper understanding of the anthropological differences between religions is at the heart of all of these conflicts. In some instances, freedom of religion entails more than simply the right to practice Navajo, or Plains, or Australian Aboriginal religion, because the underlying requirements of the practice of that religion are different.

The proper practice of a Catholic mass, for example, requires certain elements. A cross, a chalice, and sacramental wine and wafers all feature prominently, and if any of these elements was for some reason not allowed, the actual practice of Catholicism would be negatively impacted. Furthermore, it is not only native religions that limit access and place requirements on those who visit sacred spaces. Muslims, for example, should only enter the holy city of Mecca, and large parts of the Western Wall in Jerusalem are off-limits to non-Jewish people and women (Wilson 1996). Other religions place restrictions on menstruating women, and the Sikh's Golden Temple is accessible only to those who approach with covered head and bare feet (Brockman 1997). Thus, western culture is indeed familiar with and generally accepts such restrictions in the tacit acknowledgment of cultural and religious diversity. Why should Native American religion be different?

Native American religions, as land-based, also have certain requirements as well as logistical realities. If, by having Devils Tower overwhelmed with climbers you effectively remove it from Indian access during their peak ceremonial seasons, the practice of their religion is negatively impacted. Thus, First Amendment guarantees for Native Americans may in fact mean, and indeed actually require, different considerations depending on the nature of the religion itself. Certain Native American religious practices do need to be performed at Devils Tower, and only at Devils Tower. Thus, for Native Americans to have the same religious freedom as others—as guaranteed in the Constitution—due to the different requirements of the practice of their religion, different needs may in fact be appropriate.

An additional issue is the changeability of sacred space. Christianity as well as many other religions—through sanctification rituals—can create and un-create sacred space. A church that is no longer used can be deconsecrated, and torn down or converted to some other, completely secular use. Although deconsecrating a church may be unpalatable for long-term members of a congregation, the nature of the religion itself makes the act possible. The creation and un-creation of sacred land, however, is not usually an option in land-based religions. A given spot on the land was deemed sacred by creation era beings, and there is no option to deconsecrate those places (Hubert 1994).

The negotiated settlements described above for these tribal scale traditional cultural properties do not seem to put undue hardship on non-Indian visitors to these places. Certainly, their visitation comes with a number of restrictions, but overall they are not that difficult to abide by. These restrictions do impinge somewhat on Anglo behavior—by not climbing Devils Tower in June—but when the essence of Indian religious freedom is threatened by someone's recreational pursuits, it seems obvious which position should take priority (that is, the one our founding fathers put in the Constitution). To do anything less would make it difficult to believe that our nation was founded on justice for all.

Finally, the fact that native religions tend to be land-based does not necessarily mean that native peoples are unwilling to make important compromises to allow development to continue. We have seen that the temporal dimension to traditional cultural properties allows broad leeway in allowing undertakings to proceed, as does the formulation of creative, unique, case-specific mitigation measures—agreed upon through honest negotiation—that are not necessarily oriented to data recovery. As long as both or all parties in the negotiation process recognize that native peoples have genuine and legitimate concerns regarding impacts to their land-based religions as embodied in their traditional cultural properties, then compromise is possible, and a win-win outcome more likely.

Who Benefits For My Loss?

All people recognize that there are times when difficult decisions must be made, and usually, these decisions boil down to choosing the lesser of two evils. All land-altering development entails at least some degree of negative impact, and thus contains some degree of loss. The question, however, is what is gained for accepting the loss.

Traditional cultural property interviews related to projects such as uranium mine closures—something the Navajo people have wanted to see for a long, long time—will illicit particularly minimal disclosure of traditional cultural properties. In this instance the reason for such minimal disclosure is obvious: the people want the mines closed more than they want to protect their cultural properties. It is not unlikely that an interviewer could receive a response concerning the avoidance of a cultural property such as "just get the mine closed—THAT is our first priority." In this instance it is clear that the health problems of open uranium mines far outweighs any cultural benefits of avoiding even an important property. To the local Navajo community, what's the point of saving a traditional cultural property if our people get sick or die in the process? As such, depending on the nature of the undertaking itself, the results of traditional cultural property interviews may be highly varied.

If the gain is direct and immediately apparent, such as running water or electricity, then the destruction of community scale traditional cultural properties may be considered the price one has to pay, even though such properties tend to be small and can be easily avoided. Although it is untrue that asking to avoid these properties would delay or drop them from the project, the local residents appear to have already weighed the pros and cons in their own minds, and may be prepared to lose something to gain something of more immediate, tangible importance.

Perhaps the tribal government could do more public outreach to educate residents that the goal of the National Historic Preservation Act and the Section 106 process is a win-win outcome: The undertaking is completed and traditional cultural properties are not lost in the process. There may also be a lack of trust in tribal governmental promises that the avoidance of such properties will not cause a home to be dropped. Such a lack of trust may stem from longstanding tribal divisions between the pro-development nontraditional Navajo in tribal government, and the more traditionally oriented, rural residents. For community scale traditional cultural properties it is also possible that once the ceremonial event is over, it is simply culturally unnecessary to retain the actual physical manifestation of the event—for example, a Kinaaldá pit. Perhaps the nature of the ceremony itself has bearing on whether its physical manifestations should be avoided during development—for example, the physical manifestations of ceremonies other than a Kinaaldá or sweat lodges would elicit a desire to have them avoided. Perhaps it is the clustering of ceremonial locations in one area—for example, at Little Black Spot Mountain—that renders their avoidance preferable. It appears that the reasons for minimal disclosure of community scale traditional cultural properties are complex and not well understood. Nevertheless, once the desires of local individuals and communities are made clear, the undertaking may proceed even if traditional cultural properties go undocumented and are destroyed in the course of the development.

At the regional scale, where the losses may be greater and the benefits may be less obvious, the outcome is less certain. To local area residents, places like Little Black Spot Mountain are too important to ignore. In such instances it seems that balancing the benefits and losses comes out roughly even. It is here that mitigation measures can work to the benefit of both the developer and the people who must bear the negative impacts of the undertaking. It is also important to recognize that the Navajo do not generally resist development just to be difficult. As the Little Black Spot Mountain example makes clear, the local people are usually open to negotiation and compromise—even in a situation where benefits and losses are roughly equally weighted—when the party sponsoring the undertaking also negotiates and compromises in a sincere manner. A win-win outcome for all parties is the result.

When the undertaking does not directly affect local lives in a positive manner, residents are more vocal concerning the potential destruction of their traditional cultural properties, because they receive few benefits for the heavy cultural losses they incur. This may be particularly true for tribal scale traditional cultural properties that have significance to Navajo culture overall. When the negative impacts outweigh the positive impacts, people are much more likely to speak up. Such appears to be the case for the San Francisco Peaks. What benefit do the Navajo receive from the existence of the Arizona Snowbowl? There may be some minor, indirect benefits, such as some employment in service industries that cater to winter skiers, but the cultural costs involved clearly are too great for the degree of gain achieved. The nature of the impact is also relevant. Is the impact imposed from outside, by the mainstream, affluent Anglo society, or is the project sponsored by the tribal government that at least at some level has the betterment of the Navajo Nation as its goal?

The manner in which an issue is addressed is also important. In the case of the San Francisco Peaks, the Navajo felt they had little real input concerning the Forest Service's final decision. While there may indeed have been open public hearings and the Navajo may indeed have discussed the issue with Forest Service officials, they felt

Figure 7.5.   Original painting by Brandon Milford of Navajo culture in changing times. Courtesy of the Office of Navajo Government Development, Navajo Nation Government Booklet, Third Edition.

the actual outcome had been determined long before their opinions and reasons were even heard. Apparently, from the Navajo viewpoint, a few seasonal service jobs related to downhill skiing does not outweigh a feigned consultation regarding the externally driven desecration of a tribal scale traditional cultural property.

Unfortunately, the calculation of benefits and losses is not always straightforward. For minerals extraction on the reservation, external private companies certainly benefit, but so too does the Navajo Nation general fund through the payment of royalties. A healthy general fund will at least in part benefit the broader Navajo population. A further question concerns which sector benefits more from a healthy general fund. Overall, Navajo politicians—the nontraditional Navajos who live in towns—benefit the most, while the traditional, rural Navajo sector sees little of the benefit, but may bear much of the cost. Large-scale electric projects, for example, may build their transmission lines through important traditional areas, without local people even receiving electricity. As such, even internally generated developments that benefit the Navajo Nation may be protested when it is perceived that the nontraditional faction has overstepped its bounds.

It is possible that the recent higher level of consideration given to traditional cultural properties over the last decade can provide a reassessment of minerals development on the Navajo Nation. Through the long and difficult process of negotiating mitigation measures, the two broad internal divisions—the pro-development, nontraditional Navajos that dominate the Tribal Council and the traditionalists—will be brought into a place of mediation, where discussion can occur. Finally, we need to remember that the goal of the National Historic Preservation Act is not to shut down development or to preserve all cultural properties all the time. Rather, the clear goal of this important process is a win-win outcome for all.

The consideration of benefits and losses must also be understood in the broader context of current Navajo reality; that is, in the transition from a traditional society to a nontraditional one—from subsistence-based to industrial. Rather than simplistically concluding that it is all right to destroy traditional cultural properties if some personal or tribal benefit is received, it is probably more accurate to conclude that the decision is a very complex one, for difficult and profound cultural reasons. A decision of this complexity requires constant negotiation and renegotiation to find a place of balance. The balance is not simply calculating the benefits of the undertaking with the losses that could be incurred, although this is one arena in which the negotiation occurs. Rather, at a deeper level it is about finding one's balance as a Navajo in the modern world—existing in two worlds at once, each with different demands and expectations. This negotiation and renegotiation occurs both internally—almost unconsciously within each individual—and externally as a tribe, setting policies and reacting to new challenges unforeseen by their ancestors. This negotiation goes on every day, sometimes in subtle ways, as both individuals and collective Navajo culture seeks to find the best way to retain their traditional roots in this contemporary, industrial world.

Notes

1. A Fire Dance is a ceremony to aid patients who have been burned and have injuries from the trauma.

2. The National Environmental Policy Act (NEPA), passed in 1968, requires that federal agencies conduct either Environmental Assessments for smaller land-altering developments, or Environmental Impact Statements for larger land-altering developments, prior to federal undertakings.

3. "Congress shall make no law respecting an establishment of religion, or prohibiting the free exercise thereof; or abridging the freedom of speech, or of the press; or the right of the people peaceably to assemble, and to petition the Government for a redress of grievances." U.S. Constitution: First Amendment.

4. Statement by Peter Bloomer in Van Otten 1982, 22.

5. For a view of Devils Tower/Bear Lodge and further discussion of the climbing issues, see Devil's Tower National Monument, <http://www.newyoming.com/DevilsTower> (accessed February 26, 2002).

6. For a photograph of the wheel, see <http://www.kstrom.net/isk/stars/images/wheelcol.jpg> (accessed February 26, 2002).

7. For a photograph of Uluru, see "Uluru and Bald Rock: Australia's Culture and Recreation," <http://www.acn.net.au/articles/1999/06/uluru.htm> (accessed February 25, 2002).

Epilogue: Spider Woman Walks This Land

FROM THE HEIGHTS OF WHITE-CAPPED SPIDER ROCK, *Na'ashjé'ii 'Asdzáá*, Spider Woman watched as the two women drove the sandy road toward her Canyon de Chelly home in their bright red pickup truck. The July heat undulated in the air and the women had their windows rolled up and the air conditioning turned on high. The peak of summer also brought somewhere close to a hundred tourists a day to visit and photograph Spider Rock from the rim overlook run by the National Park Service. The women also knew, however, that the vast majority of the canyon bottom was off-limits to Bilagáana unless accompanied by a Navajo guide. With this assurance of privacy, at least in the immediate vicinity, the women felt unhampered as they paid a quick visit to Spider Woman.

Each woman came for different reasons. One was concerned that her young son was doing poorly in school and had taken to great misbehavior as of late. She had spoken with her son's teachers and counselors, which had helped, but she also knew that Spider Woman could influence unruly children by scaring them just a little. Certainly she didn't want her youngster's bones to wind up sun-bleached on top of Spider Woman's red rock pinnacle, but she also knew that Spider Woman was wise and could tell the difference between children that were basically good and children that really were bad. The woman knew that her son was the former. She merely wanted to ask Spider Woman for guidance, make an offering, and perhaps let Spider Woman convince her son it was in his best interest to behave.

The second woman had different thoughts in mind as they bumped along in the pickup, recently purchased brand new at the Ford dealership in Gallup. This woman was bringing her rug to Spider Rock. She wished to show Spider Woman her recently completed rug—a beautiful four by six-foot Eyedazzler woven with bright reds and greens and blues in bold, zigzagging diagonal bands. The woman wanted to thank Spider Woman for helping her with this complicated new design, since her first attempt had turned out quite well. The woman also wished to seek Spider Woman's help as she negotiated with the trader in Gallup concerning the price of her rug. Her family needed the money. The new pickup had been a bit of a stretch for them, and they were having trouble keeping up on the payments. The woman had prayed in church last Sunday to get a good price for the rug, but she thought it couldn't hurt to ask for Spider Woman's help in the matter, since after all it was she who taught the Navajo women how to weave.

The two women had been friends for many years. Indeed, two of their clans were even the same. One woman worked as a secretary at a tribal government office in Window Rock, while the other was a nurse and lived in Winslow during the week. Their children were of roughly the same ages and played together on weekends. During their younger days, both women had lived in Albuquerque and had gone to school there, but both had eventually been drawn back to the reservation as their parents had aged and needed help with the livestock.

When the women arrived at Spider Rock they pulled the pickup to the back of her tall, towering home: They instinctively knew it would be best if the Bilagáana up above were entirely out of view. Each woman pulled out a small deerskin bag full of cornmeal, and together they faced the east. Speaking softly in Navajo, each woman sprinkled a cornmeal offering toward the base of the huge, red, sandstone pinnacle. And they knew Spider Woman had heard.

References

Aberle, David. 1983a. "Peyote Religion among the Navajo." *Handbook of North American Indians: Southwest*, vol. 10, 558–69. Washington, D.C.: Smithsonian Institution Press.

———. 1983b. "Navajo Economic Development." *Handbook of North American Indians: Southwest*, vol. 10, 641–58. Washington, D.C.: Smithsonian Institution Press.

Acrey, Bill. 1998. *Navajo History: The Land and the People.* Department of Curriculum Materials Development. Shiprock, N. Mex.: Rio Grande Press.

———. 2000. *Navajo History to 1846.* Department of Curriculum Materials Development. Shiprock, N. Mex.: Rio Grande Press.

Adler, Michael, ed. 1996. *The Prehistoric Pueblo World A.D. 1150–1350.* Tucson, Ariz.: University of Arizona Press.

Advisory Council on Historic Preservation. "Tribal Historic Preservation Officers." <www.achp.gov/thpo.html>. Accessed February 24, 2002.

Anyon, Roger, T. J. Ferguson, and John Welch. 2000. "Heritage Management by American Indian Tribes in the Southwestern United States." In *Cultural Resource Management in Contemporary Society: Perspectives on Managing and Presenting the Past*, edited by Francis McManmon and Alf Hatton, 120–41. New York: Routledge.

Avallone, Ramona, Andrew Othole, and Roger Anyon. 1992. "An Archaeological and Traditional Cultural Properties Survey along Z13, Z15, and Z17 for the Proposed Zuni Wastewater Collection System Facilities." Zuni Archaeological Program Project no. ZAP-066-91. In *Zuni Archaeological Program Report No. 398.* N. Mex.: Zuni Pueblo.

Baars, Donald. 1995. *Navajo Country: A Geology and Natural History of the Four Corners Region.* Albuquerque: University of New Mexico Press.

Bailey, Garrick, and Roberta Glenn Bailey. 1986. *A History of the Navajos: The Reservation Years.* Santa Fe, N. Mex.: School of American Research Press.

Bailey, Lynn. 1964. *The Long Walk: A History of the Navajo Wars, 1846–68.* Great West and Indian Series 26. Los Angeles: Westernlore Press.

———. 1970. *Bosque Redondo: An American Concentration Camp.* Pasadena, Calif.: Socio-Technical Publications.

Banks, Kimball, Myra Giesen, and Nancy Pearson. 2000. "Traditional Cultural Properties vs. Traditional Cultural Resource Management." *Cultural Resource Management* 23, no. 1: 33–36. Washington, D.C.: U.S. Department of the Interior, National Park Service.

Bedinger, Margery. 1973. *Indian Silver: Navajo and Pueblo Jewelers.* Albuquerque, N.Mex.: University of New Mexico Press.

Begay, Richard. 1997. "The Role of Archaeology on Indian Lands: The Navajo Nation." In *Native Americans and Archaeologists: Stepping Stones to Common Ground,* edited by Nina Swidler, Kurt Dongoske, Roger Anyon, and Alan Downer, 161–66. Walnut Creek, Calif.: AltaMira Press.

Blanchard, Kendall. 1970. *The Economics of Sainthood: Religious Change among the Rimrock Navajos.* London: Associated University Presses.

Bodley, John. 1994. *Cultural Anthropology: Tribes, States, and the Global System.* Mountain View, Calif.: Mayfield Publishing.

Brock, Peggy, ed. 1989. *Women, Rites and Sites: Aboriginal Women's Cultural Knowledge.* Sydney, Australia: Allen and Unwin.

Brockman, Norbert. 1997. *Encyclopedia of Sacred Places.* Denver: ABC-CLIO.

Brugge, David. 1983. "Navajo Prehistory and History to 1850." *Handbook of North American Indians: Southwest,* vol. 10. Washington, D.C.: Smithsonian Institution Press.

———. 1994. *The Navajo–Hopi Land Dispute: An American Tragedy.* Albuquerque, N. Mex.: University of New Mexico Press.

Brugge, Doug, Timothy Benally, and Phil Harrison. 1997. *Memories Come to Us in the Wind and the Rain: Oral Histories and Photographs of Navajo Uranium Miners and Their Families.* Boston: Red Sun Press.

Carmichael, David, Jane Hubert, Brian Reeves, and Audhild Schanche, eds. 1994. *Sacred Sites, Sacred Places.* New York: Routledge.

Chamberlain, Kathleen. 1998. *Diné Bíkéyah Bik'ah (Navajo Oil): An Ethnohistory, 1922–1960.* Ph.D. Dissertation in History. Albuquerque, N. Mex.: University of New Mexico.

Choudhary, Trib. 1999. *Overall Economic Development Program, 1998–99.* Window Rock, Ariz.: Navajo Nation Division of Economic Development.

"Council OKs Gambling Law." 2001. *Navajo Times,* October 18.

"Council Rushes to Adopt Budget." 2000. *Gallup Independent,* September 8.

Cowan, James. 1992. *The Aborigine Tradition.* Shaftesbury, England: Element Books.

Dalgai, Melvin. 1995. *Power Line Extension, Telecommunications Facilities with Microwave Tower, and Access Road on Top of Little Black Spot Mountain, Piñon, Arizona.* Project Report on File (NNAD 95-029). Window Rock, Ariz.: Navajo Nation Archaeology Department.

Darlin, Darmon. 1997. "Rebellions on the Reservations." *Forbes,* May 19. <http://perc.org/newsindian.htm>. Accessed February 25, 2002.

Daugherty, John. 2000. "Dark Days on Black Mesa." <www.wildnesswithin.com/mesa.html>. Accessed February 25, 2002.

De Lacy, Terry, and Bruce Lawson. 1997. "The Uluru–Kakadu Model: Joint Management of Aboriginal-Owned National Parks in Australia." In *Conservation Through Cultural Survival: Indigenous Peoples and Protected Areas,* edited by Stan Stevens. Washington, D.C.: Island Press.

Deloria, Vine Jr., and Clifford Lytle. 1983. *American Indians, American Justice.* Austin, Tex.: University of Texas Press.

Department of the Interior, Office of American Indian Trust. 2002. "American Indians and Alaska Natives," <http:/128.174.5.51/denix/public/Native/outreach/American/indian.html>. Accessed February 24.

Devil's Tower National Monument. <www.newyoming.com/DevilsTower>. Accessed February 26, 2002.

Dobyns, Henry. 1991. "New Native World: Links between Demographic and Cultural Changes." In *Columbian Consequences: The Spanish Borderlands in Pan-American Perspective,* vol. 3, 541–60, edited by David Hurst Thomas. Washington, D.C.: Smithsonian Institution Press.

Downer, Alan. 2000. "The Navajo Nation Model: Tribal Consultation under the National Historic Preservation Act." *Cultural Resource Management* 23, no. 9: 54–56. Washington, D.C.: U.S. Department of the Interior, National Park Service, Cultural Resources.

Downs, James. [1972] 1984. *The Navajo.* Prospect Heights, Ill.: Waveland Press.

Duncan, Lois. 1996. *The Magic of Spider Woman.* New York: Scholastic.

Dussias, Allison. 1999. "Cultural Conflicts Regarding Land Use: The Conflict between Recreational Users at Devils Tower and Native American Ceremonial Users." *Vermont's Journal of the Environment.* <http://vje.org/articles/dussias2.cfm>. Accessed February 26, 2002.

Dutton, Bertha. 1976. *Navahos and Apaches: The Athabascan Peoples.* Englewood Cliffs, N.J.: Prentice-Hall.

Eichstaedt, Peter. 1994. *If You Poison Us: Uranium and Native Americans.* Santa Fe, N. Mex.: Red Crane Books.

Emerson, Gloria. 1983. "Navajo Education." *Handbook of North American Indians: Southwest,* vol. 10. Washington, D.C.: Smithsonian Institution Press.

"Ex-Navajo leader's sentence commuted." 2001. *Arizona Daily Star,* January 1.

"Families Coexist with Past, Future Threat of Uranium." 2001. *Navajo Times,* November 1.

Faris, James. 1990. *The Nightway: A History and a History of Documentation of a Navajo Ceremonial.* Albuquerque, N. Mex.: University of New Mexico Press.

Final Environmental Statement (03-04-78-01). 1979. Arizona Snow Bowl Ski Area Proposal. Coconino National Forest, USDA Forest Service, Southwestern Region, Albuquerque, New Mexico.

Forbes, Jack. 1960. *Apache, Navajo, and Spaniard.* Norman, Okla.: University of Oklahoma Press.

Frisbie, Charlotte Johnson. 1967. *Kinaaldá: A Study of the Navaho Girl's Puberty Ceremony.* Middletown, Conn.: Wesleyan University Press.

Gaming Is Official. 2001. *Navajo Times,* November 1.

Gill, Sam. 1982. *Native American Religion.* Belmont, Calif.: Wadsworth Publishing.

———. 1983. "Navajo Views of Their Origin." *Handbook of North American Indians: Southwest,* vol. 10. Washington, D.C.: Smithsonian Institution Press.

Griffin-Pierce, Trudy. 1992. *Earth Is My Mother, Sky Is My Father: Space, Time, and Astronomy in Navajo Sandpainting.* Albuquerque, N. Mex.: University of New Mexico Press.

Gulliford, Andrew. 2000. *Sacred Objects and Sacred Places: Preserving Tribal Traditions*. Denver: University of Colorado Press.

Gumerman, George. 1970. *Survey and Excavation in Northeastern Arizona, 1968*. Prescott, Ariz.: Prescott College Press.

Gumerman, George, Deborah Westfall, and Carol Weed. 1971. "Archaeological Excavations on Black Mesa, The 1969–1970 Seasons." *Prescott College Studies in Anthropology*, no. 4.

Hale, Kenneth, and David Harris. 1979. "Historical Linguistics and Archeology." *Handbook of North American Indians: Southwest*, vol. 9. Washington, D.C.: Smithsonian Institution Press.

Harvard Project on American Indian Economic Development. "Honoring Nations Division of the American Indian Economic Development Program." <http://ksgwww. harvard.edu/hpaied>. Accessed February 25, 2002.

Harvey, Sioux. 1996. "Two Models to Sovereignty: A Comparative History of the Mashantucket Pequot Tribal Nation and the Navajo Nation." *American Indian Culture and Research Journal* 20, no. 1: 147–94.

Haskell, J. Loring. 1987. *Southern Athapaskan Migration A.D. 200–1750*. Tsaile, Ariz.: Navajo Community College Press.

Henderson, Eric, and Scott Russell. 1997. "The Navajo Gaming Referendum: Reservations about Casinos Lead to Popular Rejection of Legalizing Gambling." *Human Organization* 56: 294–301.

Hester, James. 1962. "Navajo Migrations and Acculturation in the Southwest." *Museum of New Mexico Papers in Anthropology* 6.

———. 1971. *Navajo Culture Change: 1550 to 1960*. In *Apachean Culture History and Ethnology*, edited by Keith Basso and Morris Opler. Anthropological Papers of the University of Arizona 21: 51–68. Tucson, Ariz.: University of Arizona Press.

Hoijer, Harry. 1971. *The Position of the Apachean Languages in the Athapaskan Stock*. In *Apachean Culture History and Ethnology*, edited by Keith Basso and Morris Opler. Anthropological Papers of the University of Arizona 21: 3–6. Tucson, Ariz.: University of Arizona Press.

Holt, Barry. 1990. *Tribal Sovereignty over Archaeology: A Practical and Legal Fact*. In *Preservation on the Reservation: Native Americans, Native American Lands and Archaeology*, edited by Anthony Klesert and Alan Downer, 9–25. Navajo Nation Papers in Anthropology, no. 26. Window Rock, Ariz.: Navajo Nation Archaeology Department.

"Homes Near Old Mines Made of Uranium Bricks." 2000. *Gallup Independent*, November 13.

Hubert, Jane. 1994. "Sacred Beliefs and Beliefs of Sacredness." In *Sacred Sites, Sacred Places*, edited by David Carmichael, Jane Hubert, Brian Reeves, and Audhild Schanche, 257–64. New York: Routledge.

Indian Land Claims Settlements. Legal Information Institute: U.S. Code Collection. <www4.law.cornell.edu/uscode/25/ch19.html>. Accessed February 24, 2002.

Iverson, Peter. 1983. "The Emerging Navajo Nation." *Handbook of North American Indians: Southwest*, vol. 10. Washington, D.C.: Smithsonian Institution Press.

Jett, Stephen. 1974. "The Destruction of Navajo Orchards in 1864: Captain John Thompson's Report." *Arizona and the West* 16: 365–78.

———. 1993. "An Introduction to Navajo Sacred Places." *Journal of Cultural Geography* 1993: 29–39.

———. 1995. "Navajo Sacred Places: Management and Interpretation of Mythic History." *The Public Historian* 17, no. 2: 39–47.

Jett, Stephen, and Virgini Spencer. 1981. *Navajo Architecture: Forms, History, Distributions.* Tucson, Ariz.: University of Arizona Press.

Joe, Jennie. 1998. "The Impact of Relocation on Hardrock Chapter." In *Diné Bíkéyah: Papers in Honor of David M. Brugge,* edited by Meliha Duran and David Kirkpatrick. Archaeological Society of New Mexico 24: 129–41.

Johnson, Broderick, ed. 1973. *Navajo Stories of the Long Walk Period.* Tsaile, Ariz.: Navajo Community College Press.

Kahlenberg, Mary Hunt, and Anthony Berlant. 1972. *The Navajo Blanket.* New York: Praeger Publishers.

Kappler, Charles, ed. 1972. *Indian Treaties, 1778–1883.* New York: Interland Publishing.

Kelley, Klara Bonsack, and Harris Francis. 1994. *Navajo Sacred Places.* Bloomington, Ind.: Indiana University Press.

———. 1998. "Anthropological Traditions Versus Navajo Traditions in Early Navajo History." In *Diné Bíkéyah: Papers in Honor of David M. Brugge,* edited by Meliha Duran and David Kirkpatrick. Archaeological Society of New Mexico 24:143–55.

Kelley, Klara Bonsack, and Peter Whiteley. 1989. *Navajoland: Family, Settlement and Land Use.* Tsaile, Ariz.: Navajo Community College Press.

Kessell, John. 1989. "Spaniards and Pueblos: From Crusading Intolerance to Pragmatic Accommodation." In *Columbian Consequences: The Spanish Borderlands in Pan-American Perspective,* vol. 1, edited by David Hurst Thomas, 127–38. Washington, D.C.: Smithsonian Institution Press.

Keur, Dorothy. 1944. "A Chapter in Navajo–Pueblo Relations." *American Antiquity* 10, no. 1: 75–86.

King, Thomas F. 1998. *Cultural Resource Laws and Practice: An Introductory Guide.* Walnut Creek, Calif.: AltaMira Press.

Klesert, Anthony. 1990. "Contracting Federal Historic Preservation Functions under the Indian Self-Determination Act." In *Preservation on the Reservation: Native Americans, Native American Lands and Archaeology,* edited by Anthony Klesert and Alan Downer. Navajo Nation Papers in Anthropology, no. 26. Window Rock, Ariz.: Navajo Nation Archaeology Department.

Klesert, Anthony, and Alan Downer, eds. 1990. "Preservation on the Reservation: Native Americans, Native American Lands, and Archaeology." *Navajo Nation Papers in Anthropology,* no. 26. Window Rock, Ariz.: Navajo Nation Archaeology Department.

Kluckhohn, Clyde, W. Hill, and Lucy Kluckhohn. 1971. *Navaho Material Culture.* Cambridge, Mass.: Belknap Press of Harvard University Press.

Lapanie, Harrison, Jr. 2002. "U.S. Treaty with the Navajos." <www.lapahie.com/ Dine_Treaty.html>. Accessed February 24.

Linford, Laurance. 2000. *Navajo Places: History, Legend, Landscape.* Salt Lake City, Utah: University of Utah Press.

"Local Groups Hail Removal of Uranium Mining Research Funding." 2001. *Navajo Times*, November 21.

Lockyard, Louise. 1995. "New Paper Words: Historical Images of Navajo Language Literacy." *American Indian Quarterly* 19, no. 1: 17–30.

Mails, Thomas, and Dan Evehema. 1995. *Hotevilla: Hopi Shrine of the Covenant, Microcosm of the World.* New York: Marlowe and Co.

Martin, Rena. 1997. "How Traditional Navajos View Historic Preservation: A Question of Interpretation." In *Native Americans and Archaeologists: Stepping Stones to Common Ground*, edited by Nina Swidler, Kurt Dongoske, Roger Anyon, and Alan Downer, 128–34. Walnut Creek, Calif.: AltaMira Press.

Matthews, Washington. 1902. "The Night Chant: A Navaho Ceremony." Publications of the Hyde Southwestern Expedition. In *Memoirs of the American Museum of Natural History*, Whole Series Volume 6 (Anthropology Series Volume 5). New York: AMS Press.

———. 1994. *Navaho Legends.* Salt Lake City, Utah: University of Utah Press.

McManamon, Francis, ed. 1999. "Preservation on the Reservation [and Beyond]." *Common Ground: Archaeology and Ethnography in the Public Interest*, Fall 1999. Washington, D.C.: National Park Service.

McNitt, Frank. 1972. *Navajo Wars: Military Campaigns, Slave Raids and Reprisals.* Albuquerque, N. Mex.: University of New Mexico Press.

McPherson, Robert. 1992a. "Sacred Land Sacred View: Navajo Perceptions of the Four Corners Region." *Charles Redd Monographs in Western History* 19. Provo, Utah: Brigham Young University.

———. 1992b. "Naaléhé Bá Hooghan—House of Merchandise: The Navajo Trading Post as an Institution of Cultural Change, 1900–1930." *American Indian Culture and Research Journal* 16, no. 1: 23–43.

"Meetings Detail Uranium Law." 2000. *Gallup Independent*, August 14.

Milne, Courtney. 1995. *Sacred Places in North America: A Journey into the Medicine Wheel.* New York: Stewart, Tabori and Chang.

Mullett, G. M. 1979. *Spider Woman Stories: Legends of the Hopi Indians.* Tucson, Ariz.: University of Arizona Press.

Nafziger, Richard. 1980. "Transnational Energy Corporations and American Indian Development." In *American Indian Energy Resources and Development*, edited by Roxanne Dunbar Ortiz. Albuquerque, N. Mex.: Institute for Native American Development, Native American Studies, University of New Mexico.

National Native American Graves Protection and Repatriation Act (NAGPRA) Database. National NAGPRA: National Park Service, National Center for Cultural Resources. <www.cast.uark.edu/other/nps/nagpra>. Accessed February 24, 2002.

National Park Service. 2001. "Rainbow Bridge National Monument." <www.nps.gov/rabr>. Accessed February 25, 2002.

———. 2002a. "Register of Historic Places." <www.cr.nps.gov/nr/>. Accessed February 24.

———. 2002b. Secretary of the Interior's Standards and Guidelines for Federal Agency Historic Preservation Programs Pursuant to the National Historic Preservation Assistance Program. <www2.cr.nps.gov/pad/sec110.htm>. Accessed February 24, 2002.

National Tribal Development Association. 2002. "A Tribal Governance Leap into a New Millennium." <www.ntda.rockyboy.org>. Accessed February 25.

"Navajo Budget Bigger." 2000. *Navajo Nation Messenger*, September 6.

Navajo Nation Archaeology Department. 2002. <http://www.navajo.org/archaeology>. Accessed February 26, 2002.

Navajo Nation Preservation Roads Planning Program, Navajo Nation Historic Preservation Department. <http://hpd.navajo.org>. Accessed February 25, 2002.

Navajo Rugs of Hubbell Trading Post National Historic Site, Southwest Parks and Monuments Association. <http://navajorugs.spma.org>.

"Navajos join forces with Sandia Lab." 2000. *Arizona Daily Star*, December 15.

Newcomb, Franc Johnson. 1990. *Navaho Folk Tales*. Albuquerque, N. Mex.: University of New Mexico Press.

"New Report by NRDC Shows Material Damage to N-Aquifer." 2000. *The Hopi Tutuveni*, October 31.

Nugent, John Peer. 1975. "The Chairman of Navajo Inc." *Signature* (December 1975), vertical file: Peter MacDonald. Gallup Public Library. Gallup, Mew Mexico.

O'Bryan, Aileen. 1956. *The Diné: Origin Myths of the Navaho Indians*. Washington, D.C.: U.S. Government Printing Office.

"Officials Seek Traditional Medicineman Apprentices." 2000. *Navajo Times*, August 10.

Ortiz, David. 1999. "Road Project Ethnography: Observations on the Role of the Anthropologist and the Cultural Specialist." In *Diné Baa Hané Bi Naaltsoos: Collected Papers from the Seventh through Tenth Navajo Studies Conferences*, edited by June-el Piper, 51–61. Window Rock, Ariz.: Navajo Nation Historic Preservation Department.

Oswalt, Wendell, and Sharlotte Neely. 1998. *This Land Was Theirs: A Study of North American Indians*. Mountain View, Calif.: Mayfield.

Oughton, Jerrie. 1994. *The Magic Weaver of Rugs: A Tale of the Navajo*. Boston: Houghton Mifflin.

"Out of Balance." 2000. *Navajo Times*, December 27.

Parker, Patricia, ed. 1993. "Traditional Cultural Properties." *Cultural Resource Management* 16, Special Issue. Washington, D.C.: U.S. Department of the Interior, National Park Service.

Parker, Patricia, and Thomas King. 1998. "Guidelines for Evaluating and Documenting Traditional Cultural Properties." *National Register Bulletin* 38. Washington, D.C.: U.S. Department of the Interior, National Park Service.

Patterson, Alex. 1992. "A Field Guide to Rock Art Symbols of the Greater Southwest." Boulder, Co.: Johnson Books.

"Plan to sell alcohol at casino stirs a caution." 2000. *Arizona Daily Star*, November 26.

Powers, Margaret, and Byron Johnson. 1987. Defensive Sites of Dinétah. *Cultural Resources Series*, no. 2. Albuquerque, N.Mex.: U.S. Department of the Interior, Bureau of Land Management.

Preston, Douglas. 1995. *Talking to the Ground: One Family's Journey on Horseback across the Sacred Land of the Navajo*. Albuquerque, N. Mex.: University of New Mexico Press.

Price, Nicole. 1994. "Tourism and the Bighorn Medicine Wheel: How Multiple Use Does Not Work for Sacred Sites." In *Sacred Sites, Sacred Places*, edited by David Carmichael, Jane Hubert, Brian Reeves, and Audhild Schanche, 257–64. New York: Routledge.

Prucha, Francis. 1979. *The Churches and the Indian Schools, 1888–1912.* Lincoln, Nebr.: University of Nebraska Press.

Pynes, Patrick. 1999. "Extraction or Reciprocation? Conflict over the Navajo Nation's Ponderosa Pine Forests." In *Diné Baa Hané Bi Naaltsoos: Collected Papers from the Seventh through Tenth Navajo Studies Conferences,* edited by June-el Piper, 157–65. Window Rock, Ariz.: Navajo Nation Historic Preservation Department.

"Radioactive Reservation." 2000. *Arizona Daily Star,* July 30.

Rappaport, Roy. 2001. *Ecology and the Sacred: Engaging the Anthropology of Roy A. Rappaport.* Ann Arbor, Mich.: University of Michigan Press.

Reed, Alan. 1987. "A Technique for Ranking Prehistoric Sites in Terms of Scientific Significance." *American Archaeology* 6, no. 2: 127–30.

Reff, Daniel. 1991. *Disease, Depopulation, and Culture Change in Northwestern New Spain, 1518–1764.* Salt Lake City, Utah: University of Utah Press.

Reichard, Gladys. [1934] 1997. *Spider Woman: A Story of Navajo Weavers and Chanters.* Albuquerque, N. Mex.: University of New Mexico Press.

Reinhart, Theodore. 1999. "The Trader and Navajo Culture Change." In *Diné Baa Hané Bi Naaltsoos: Collected Papers from the Seventh through Tenth Navajo Studies Conferences,* edited by June-el Piper, 97–103. Window Rock, Ariz.: Navajo Nation Historic Preservation Department, Window Rock.

Reno, Philip. 1981. *Mother Earth, Father Sky, and Economic Development: Navajo Resources and Their Use.* Albuquerque, N. Mex.: University of New Mexico Press.

Ritchie, David. 1994. "Principles and Practice of Site Protection Laws in Australia." *In Sacred Sites, Sacred Places,* edited by David Carmichael, Jane Hubert, Brian Reeves, and Audhild Schanche, 224–27. New York: RoutledgeRodee, Marian. 1977. *Southwestern Weaving.* Albuquerque, N. Mex.: University of New Mexico Press.

Roessel, Ruth. 1983. "Navajo Arts and Crafts." *Handbook of North American Indians: Southwest,* vol. 10. Washington, D.C.: Smithsonian Institution Press.

Russell, Scott. 1999. "Contemporary Navajo Wage Labor and Income Patterns." In *Diné Baa Hané Bi Naaltsoos: Collected Papers from the Seventh through Tenth Navajo Studies Conferences,* edited by June-el Piper, 147–55. Window Rock, Ariz.: Navajo Nation Historic Preservation Department, Window Rock.

Salerno, Sal. 1993. "Medicine Wheel Agreement Set Historic Precedent for Protection of Sacred Sites." *News from Indian Country: Mid-August 1993.*

Scarborough, Robert. 1981. *Radioactive Occurrences of Uranium Production in Arizona.* Tucson, Ariz.: Arizona Bureau of Geology and Mineral Technology, Geological Survey Branch.

Shapiro, Joseph. 1988. "Up by the Bootstraps is an Uphill Fight for Indians." *U.S. News and World Report,* 22 February, 26–27.

Shepardson, Mary. 1983. "Development of Navajo Tribal Government." *Handbook of North American Indians: Southwest,* vol. 10. Washington, D.C.: Smithsonian Institution Press.

Skinner, Charles. 1896. *Myths and Legends of Our Own Land.* Philadelphia: J.P. Lippincott.

Smith, Huston, and Reuben Snake. 1996. *One Nation Under God: The Triumph of the Native American Church.* Santa Fe, N. Mex.: Clear Light Publishers.

Spurr, Kimberly. 1993. "NAGPRA and Archaeology on Black Mesa, Arizona." *Navajo Nation Papers in Anthropology* 30. Window Rock, Ariz.: Navajo Nation Archaeology Department.

Stoffle, Richard, and Michael Evans. 1990. "Holistic Conservation and Cultural Triage: American Indian Perspectives on Cultural Resources." *Human Organization* 49, no. 2: 91–99.

Tarlock, Dan A. 1999. "Australian and United States Law of Aboriginal Land Rights: A Comparative Perspective." *Vermont's Journal of the Environment.* <http://vje.org/articles/tarlock.html>. Accessed February 26, 2002.

Terrell, John Upton. 1970. *The Navajos: The Past and Present of a Great People.* New York: Weybright and Talley.

Thompson, Kerry, and Ettie Anderson. 1999. *An Archaeological Survey of the Cameron 5 Abandoned Mine Lands Reclamation Project near Cameron, Arizona.* Window Rock, Ariz.: Flagstaff Office, Navajo Nation Archaeology Department, Report No. 99–50.

Tolan, Sandy. 1989. "Showdown at Window Rock." *New York Times Magazine,* November 26, 28–37.

Towner, Ronald. 1996. *The Archaeology of Navajo Origins.* Salt Lake City, Utah: University of Utah Press.

Trafzer, Clifford. 1982. *The Kit Carson Campaign: The Last Great Navajo War.* Norman, Okla.: University of Oklahoma Press.

Two Bears, Davina. 1999. "Navajos Learning and Doing Archaeology: Navajo Nation Archaeology Department's Student Training Program at Northern Arizona University." In *Diné Baa Hané Bi Naaltsoos: Collected Papers from the Seventh through Tenth Navajo Studies Conferences,* edited by June-el Piper, 4750. Window Rock, Ariz.: Navajo Nation Historic Preservation Department.

Uluru and Bald Rock. "Australia's Culture and Recreation." 2002. <http://www.acn.net.au/articles/1999/06/uluru.htm>. Accessed February 25, 2002.

Underhill, Ruth. 1956. *The Navajos.* Norman, Okla.: University of Oklahoma Press.

U.S. Department of Education. 1990. "The *Diné* of the Eastern Region of the Navajo Reservation." In *Oral History Stories of the Long Walk Hwéeldi Baa Hané.* Washington, D.C.

U.S. Department of the Interior. Indian Trust Management Information. <www.doi.gov>. Accessed February 25, 2002.

Van Otten, George, ed. 1982. *Respecting a Mountain.* Proceedings of the Arizona Humanities Council, Northern Arizona University, Department of Geography, 1982 Forum on the Development of the Arizona Snowbowl on the San Francisco Peaks, Arizona.

Van Valkenburgh, Richard. 1974. *Navajo Sacred Places.* New York: Garland Publishing.

Warburton, Miranda. 2000. "Who's Program Is It, Anyway?" *High Plains Applied Anthropologist* 1, no. 20: 96–99.

Warburton, Miranda, and Richard Begay. 2000. "Navajo and Anasazi—What Is the Relationship?" Manuscript on file with author.

Ward, Albert. 1980. "An Archaeological Reflection of Ethnographic Reality." *Ethnohistorical Report Series* No. 2. Albuquerque, N. Mex.: Center for Anthropological Studies.

Waters, Frank. 1950. *Masked Gods: Navajo and Pueblo Ceremonialism.* Chicago: Swallow Press.

Weiger, Pamela. 1998. "*Diné College* Folds Unique Navajo Philosophy into Its Class Curriculum." *Community College Week* 11, no. 7:16–18.

Welfare Program in Tribal Hands. 2000. *Gallup Independent,* September 9.

"What They're Saying about EZs." 2002. <www.urich.edu/~ezproj/april99/what.htm>. Accessed February 25.

Wilkins, David. 1999. *The Navajo Political Experience*. Tsaile, Ariz.: Diné College Press.

Wilson, Alan, and Gene Dennison. 1995. *Navajo Place Names: An Observer's Guide*. Guilford, Conn.: Jeffery Norton Publishers.

Wilson, Colin. 1996. *The Atlas of Holy Places and Sacred Sites*. London: Dorling Kindersley.

Wilson, John. 1990. "We've Got Thousands of These!" What Makes an Historic Farmstead Significant? *Historical Archaeology* 24: 23–33.

Witherspoon, Gary. 1983. "Language and Reality in Navajo World View." *Handbook of North American Indians: Southwest*, vol. 10. Washington, D. C.: Smithsonian Institution Press.

Wyman, Leland. 1970. "Blessingway." Tucson, Ariz.: University of Arizona Press.

———. 1983. Navajo Ceremonial System. *Handbook of North American Indians: Southwest*, vol.10. Washington, D.C.: Smithsonian Institution Press.

Yazzie, Sonya. 1999. "Lifestyle Changes among the Navajo: A Cause of Diabetes." In *Diné Baa Hané Bi Naaltsoos: Collected Papers from the Seventh through Tenth Navajo Studies Conferences*, edited by June-el Piper, 119–24. Window Rock, Ariz.; Navajo Nation Historic Preservation Department.

Young, Robert, and William Morgan. 1987. *The Navajo Language: A Grammar and Colloquial Dictionary*. Albuquerque, N. Mex.: University of New Mexico Press.

Zolbrod, Paul. 1984. *Diné Bahane,'The Navajo Creation Story*. Albuquerque, N. Mex.: University of New Mexico Press.

Index

About the Author

Kelli Carmean has taught anthropology and archaeology to undergraduates at Eastern Kentucky University since 1993. She has a Ph.D. from the University of Pittsburgh, where she wrote a dissertation concerning Sayil, an archaeological site in Mexico's Yucatan peninsula. Her undergraduate degree is also in anthropology, from the University of Victoria, in British Columbia, Canada. Dr. Carmean has participated in archaeological investigations in Canada, Israel, Mexico, Peru, and the United States. She continues to enjoy traveling, and has taught anthropology in a variety of study abroad programs, including in Australia, China, Ecuador, and Mexico.